Pre Law Best Mode Strategies to Win Before Law School Even Begins

Joseline Jean-Louis Hardrick

Published by Lawyerish®, 2025.

PRE LAW BEST MODE STRATEGIES TO WIN BEFORE LAW SCHOOL EVEN BEGINS

First edition. August 29, 2025.

Copyright © 2025 Joseline Jean-Louis Hardrick.

ISBN: 978-1958912713

Written by Joseline Jean-Louis Hardrick.

Table of Contents

"A lawyer is either a social engineer or a parasite on society."

– Charles Hamilton Houston

Prologue

Over the years, I've had the honor of walking alongside hundreds of students and reaching thousands more as both a law professor and as the founder of Journey to Esquire® and Lawyerish®.

My classrooms, workshops, and community programs have given me a front row seat to the dreams, struggles, setbacks, and triumphs of aspiring lawyers. I've seen firsthand how the path to law school—and through it—can be both exhilarating and exhausting.

The stories you will find in this book are drawn from that wealth of experience. The names, characters, and situations are a compilation of many different individuals and their journeys. They are not meant to represent any one particular person. I take confidentiality very seriously, and while these stories are inspired by real people and real struggles, they have been shaped to protect privacy while still revealing the truth of what it means to prepare for law school and step into your calling.

Beyond teaching, I also offer one-on-one coaching and mentorship as The Law School Pro™, helping students build confidence, strategy, and resilience. I've written multiple books on law school, wellness, and success, and I create documentaries, blogs, and other forms of media with one goal in mind: to reach and empower people who feel called to the law.

This book is my invitation to you: step into BEST MODE. Take the lessons of those who came before you, weave them into your own journey, and get ready to transform not just your career, but your life.

Chapter 1: Introduction

Why Wait? Start Great

Law school isn't just a three-year commitment—it's a complete lifestyle shift that begins long before you ever set foot in a classroom. Think about it: by the time most students walk through those law school doors, they've already experienced months (or even years) of stress preparing for the LSAT, crafting applications, and anxiously waiting for acceptance letters.

Here's something most pre-law advisors won't tell you: about 80% of law school stress actually begins before you even apply. The anxiety, self-doubt, and overwhelming pressure don't magically appear during orientation—they've been building throughout your undergraduate years as you worry about your GPA, extracurriculars, and whether you're "law school material."

This is exactly why I created the BE§T MODE Mindset. What does BE§T MODE stand for? It's about the following actions that keep you focused and motivated:

- Believe in Your Calling
- Eliminate the Distractions
- Set the Foundation Early & Strategize
- Train for the LSAT
- Master Your Mindset
- Open Doors Before Closing
- Design your Health strategy
- Elevate Your application game

. It's a complete operating system for approaching your pre-law journey with confidence and strategic planning rather than panic and last-minute cramming.

Let me be clear: this book isn't about adding more to your already full plate. It's about saving you from unnecessary "stress debt" and drama. Just like financial debt can follow you for years, accumulated stress can impact your performance, health, and happiness throughout law school and beyond.

The BE§T MODE approach is designed to help you work smarter, not harder. By starting early and approaching your pre-law journey strategically, you'll avoid the common pitfalls that trap so many aspiring lawyers. You'll learn to build habits that serve you not just in getting accepted to law school, but in thriving once you're there.

Throughout this book, I'll guide you through practical strategies for everything from managing your GPA and preparing for the LSAT to crafting standout applications and maintaining your physical and mental health. These aren't just nice-to-have suggestions, they're essential components of a successful pre-law journey.

So why wait until senior year panic sets in? Why not start great now? By embracing the BE§T MODE Mindset early, you'll transform what could be years of anxiety into a purposeful journey toward becoming the lawyer you're meant to be.

Let's get started.

Chapter 2: Believe in Your Calling

Finding Your Why

The path to law school is challenging, there's no way around it. When the LSAT questions seem impossible, when your personal statement draft gets torn apart, or when you're questioning if you can afford another year of education, you'll need something stronger than just "wanting to be a lawyer" to keep you going.

This is where your "why" comes in.

Your "why" is your personal connection to the law—the reason that pulls you toward this profession even when the path gets tough. It's deeper than "I want a good salary" or "My parents expect me to go to law school." Those external motivations rarely sustain you through the challenges ahead.

Take a moment to ask yourself: What truly draws me to the legal profession? Maybe you witnessed injustice in your community and want to create change. Perhaps you're fascinated by how laws shape society. Or maybe your analytical mind loves solving complex problems.

Whatever your reason, write it down. Make it specific and personal. Here's an exercise to help you clarify your "why":

- Complete this sentence: "I want to become a lawyer because..."
- Then ask yourself "Why is that important to me?"
- Answer that question, then ask "Why?" again.
- Repeat this process 3-5 times, digging deeper each time.

This "Five Whys" technique often reveals motivations you hadn't fully articulated before. One student I worked with started with "I want to become a lawyer because I'm good at arguing." After several "whys," she discovered her deeper motivation: "I want to advocate for children in the foster care system because I grew up in that system and saw how much difference a good advocate can make."

That's a "why" that can sustain you through late-night study sessions and disappointing test scores.

Your "why" also helps you set professional goals. Are you drawn to corporate law, public interest, criminal defense, or another specialty? While you don't need to have your entire career mapped out, having a general direction helps you make strategic choices during your pre-law journey.

Remember, your "why" may evolve over time and that's perfectly okay. The important thing is having that north star to guide you when the path gets foggy.

Beyond LSAT Scores

LET'S TALK ABOUT THE elephant in the pre-law room: the LSAT. For many aspiring lawyers, this test becomes the center of their universe, the sole measure of their potential success.

But here's the truth: you are so much more than a test score.

While the LSAT is important (and we'll talk about preparing for it in Chapter 5), fixating solely on your score can blind you to the bigger picture of your legal journey. The most successful law students and lawyers aren't necessarily those with the highest LSAT scores, they're the ones who develop a complete set of skills and a resilient mindset.

Visualization is a powerful tool for seeing beyond test scores. Try this exercise: Close your eyes and imagine yourself three years from now, walking across the stage at your law school graduation. What qualities helped you succeed? Probably not just your test-taking abilities, but also your perseverance, your critical thinking, your ability to build relationships, and your passion for the law.

Now imagine yourself five years after that, thriving in your legal career. What are you doing? Who are you helping? How does it feel to be making an impact through your work?

This kind of visualization helps you connect your current efforts to your future success in a way that transcends any single test or application component.

Consider Maria, a student who scored lower than she hoped on her first LSAT practice test. Instead of giving up, she visualized herself as a successful immigration attorney, helping families like her own. This vision gave her the motivation to improve her score, but more importantly, it reminded her that the LSAT was just one step in her journey, not the destination itself.

Or take James, who struggled with standardized tests due to anxiety but excelled in mock trial competitions. By visualizing himself as a trial attorney using his public speaking skills to advocate for clients, he maintained perspective when his LSAT preparation became challenging.

Your legal journey is a marathon, not a sprint. The LSAT is just one mile marker along the way—important, yes, but not definitive of your worth or potential as a lawyer.

Affirmations for Future Lawyers

THE VOICE IN YOUR HEAD has tremendous power. When that voice says, "I don't belong in law school" or "I'm not smart enough for this," it creates real obstacles to your success. Countering these negative thoughts with positive affirmations isn't just feel-good fluff—it's a practical strategy for building the confidence you'll need throughout your legal career.

Affirmations work best when they're specific to your journey. Here are some tailored for pre-law students:

- "I am developing the analytical skills needed for legal success."
- "My unique perspective will be valuable in the legal profession."
- "I handle challenges with determination and grace."
- "I am worthy of my law school dreams."
- "Each day, I'm becoming more prepared for my legal future."

Choose one or two that resonate with you, or create your own. The key is to make them present-tense, positive statements that feel authentic when you say them.

For these affirmations to truly take root, pair them with a regular journaling practice. Try these prompts:

- What small win did I experience today that shows I'm developing as a future lawyer?
- What challenge did I face, and how did overcoming it make me stronger?
- What unique quality do I possess that will serve me well in the legal profession?
- How did I show up for myself today in my pre-law journey?

Journaling helps reinforce your affirmations by connecting them to real experiences in your life. It also creates a record of your growth that you can look back on during difficult times.

Consider Jasmine, who started each morning by writing "I am building the skills and confidence to become an exceptional attorney" in her journal. When she received a disappointing grade in her constitutional law class, she reviewed her journal and saw months of evidence of her growth and resilience. This perspective helped her bounce back quickly and improve her performance.

The journey to becoming a lawyer will test your confidence repeatedly. Building a practice of positive self-talk now creates a foundation of self-belief that will support you through law school applications, 1L year, bar exam preparation, and beyond.

Your mind is your most powerful asset as a future lawyer. Train it to be your ally, not your critic.

Morning Practice: Begin each day by reading one affirmation aloud, then taking a moment to truly feel its meaning.

Targeted Support: Select specific affirmations that address your current challenges or doubts.

Visual Reminders: Print our affirmations on index cards and place them where you'll see them regularly: on your desk, bathroom mirror, or inside your planner.

Journaling Prompts: Use these affirmations as starting points for deeper reflection in your journal.

Stress Response: When anxiety or self-doubt arises, reach for a relevant affirmation card to reset your mindset.

Remember that affirmations work best when they feel authentic and connected to your values. Modify these statements to use language that resonates with you personally.

Chapter 3: Eliminate the Distractions

Social Media Boundaries

Let's be honest: social media can be both a blessing and a curse for pre-law students. On one hand, it connects you with valuable communities, information, and opportunities. On the other hand, it can become a black hole of comparison, distraction, and wasted time.

The goal isn't to abandon social media completely—that's neither realistic nor necessary. Instead, you need boundaries that allow you to use these platforms intentionally without letting them hijack your focus and emotional wellbeing.

Start by auditing your current social media habits. For one week, track:

- How much time you spend on each platform?
- When you typically check social media?
- How you feel before, during, and after scrolling?
- What value (if any) you get from each session?

This awareness alone often leads to natural adjustments in behavior. You might notice that your 10-minute "quick check" of Instagram regularly turns into an hour-long scroll session, or that checking Twitter before bed leaves you feeling anxious and unable to sleep.

Based on your audit, create specific boundaries that address your personal pitfalls. For example:

- No social media until after you've completed your morning study session.

- A 30-minute time limit for all social media use during weekdays.
- No phones in the bedroom to prevent late-night scrolling.
- Designated "social media free" days each week.

Use technology to support your boundaries. Most smartphones now have screen time limits and app blocking features. Tools like Freedom, Forest, and Focus@Will can help you create distraction-free work periods.

While limiting consumption, be strategic about your own social media presence. Many law schools look at applicants' social media profiles, and your future employers certainly will. Use these platforms to showcase your professional interests and community involvement rather than posting content you might later regret.

Consider creating a separate professional account on platforms like Twitter or LinkedIn where you can follow law schools, legal organizations, and attorneys in your areas of interest. This transforms social media from a distraction into a valuable networking and learning tool.

Consider Carlos, who found himself constantly distracted by social media notifications while studying. He implemented a "phone in another room" policy during study sessions and saw his productivity double. He also set up a professional Twitter account where he followed legal news sources and engaged with content related to his interest in environmental law—an activity that actually enhanced his law school applications.

The key is intentionality. Social media isn't inherently good or bad—it's how you use it that matters. With thoughtful boundaries, you can enjoy the benefits while protecting your time, focus, and mental health.

Identifying Energy Vampires

YOU'VE PROBABLY EXPERIENCED this: after spending time with certain people, you feel drained, discouraged, or doubtful about your law school plans. These are what I call "energy vampires"—people who, intentionally or not, suck the motivation and confidence right out of you.

Energy vampires in the pre-law world come in many forms:

- The constant competitor who turns every conversation into a

comparison of LSAT scores or application status.
- The doom-and-gloom friend who only shares horror stories about law school debt and lawyer burnout.
- The dismissive family member who questions whether you're "cut out" for law school.
- The distraction buddy who always tempts you away from studying.
- The advice over loader who overwhelms you with contradictory suggestions.

The first step in dealing with energy vampires is simply recognizing them. Pay attention to how you feel after interactions. Do you feel energized and supported, or depleted and doubtful? Your emotional response is a reliable indicator of whether someone is adding to or subtracting from your pre-law journey.

Once you've identified the energy vampires in your life, you have several options for creating healthy distance:

Set conversation boundaries. When your cousin starts questioning your law school choices at family dinner, try: "I appreciate your concern, but I've done my research and feel confident in my path. Let's talk about something else."

Limit exposure. You don't need to cut people off completely, but you can reduce the time you spend with those who drain you. Schedule shorter coffee dates instead of long dinners, or meet in groups rather than one-on-one.

Be selective about what you share. Not everyone needs to know your LSAT score or which schools you're applying to. Save those conversations for people who have proven themselves supportive.

Find your tribe. Actively seek out people who energize and support you—fellow pre-law students who lift each other up, mentors who offer constructive guidance, or friends who believe in your dreams.

Consider one student I mentored who found herself avoiding LSAT prep because her roommate constantly made anxiety-inducing comments about how hard the test was. She started studying at the library instead of at home and joined a supportive online LSAT study group. Her practice scores improved within weeks.

Creating distance from energy vampires isn't selfish, it's necessary self-preservation. The path to law school is challenging enough without carrying the additional weight of others' negativity or doubt.

This doesn't mean surrounding yourself only with yes-people who never challenge you. Constructive criticism from supportive sources is valuable. The difference is in the intent and impact: does this person want to see you succeed and leave you feeling capable of improvement, or do they leave you feeling inadequate and discouraged?

Choose your company wisely. Your law school dreams are too important to be derailed by energy vampires.

Creating A Focus First Environment

YOUR ENVIRONMENT SHAPES your focus, productivity, and ultimately, your success. Creating spaces that prioritize concentration isn't just about tidying up, it's about designing your physical and digital worlds to make focus the path of least resistance.

Let's start with your physical study space. Whether it's a dedicated home office, a dorm room desk, or a favorite library corner, your ideal study environment should:

Minimize visual distractions (clear surfaces, organized materials)

Support good posture and physical comfort

Have adequate lighting to prevent eye strain

Include all necessary materials within arm's reach

Signal to your brain "this is where work happens"

Personalize your space with small touches that motivate you—perhaps a plant, an inspiring quote, or a photo that reminds you of your "why." But be careful not to overcrowd with distractions.

Your digital environment needs just as much attention. Consider:

- Organizing files into a logical system so you don't waste time searching.
- Using browser extensions like StayFocusd or LeechBlock to limit access to distracting websites during study hours.
- Creating separate user profiles or browsers for school work versus

personal browsing

- Setting up email filters to prioritize important messages.
- Using project management tools like Trello or Notion to keep track of application deadlines and study schedules.

The most effective focus environments also address sound. Some people work best in complete silence, while others need background noise. Experiment to find what works for you. Noise-cancelling headphones and apps like Noisli or Brain.fm can help create your ideal sound environment regardless of where you're studying.

Don't forget about your phone, perhaps the biggest focus disruptor of all. During dedicated study sessions, try:

- Putting your phone in another room.
- Using apps like Forest that "grow" virtual trees while you stay off your phone.
- Turning on Do Not Disturb mode.
- Placing your phone in a timed lock box (yes, these exist!).

Consider Marcus, who transformed his mediocre study habits by creating a "focus zone" in the corner of his apartment. He removed all electronics except his laptop, added a good lamp and comfortable chair, and hung a small whiteboard for tracking LSAT practice scores. This dedicated space helped him mentally transition into study mode, and his consistency improved dramatically.

Your environment should also support task transitions. Consider creating "start-up" and "shut-down" routines that signal to your brain when it's time to focus and when it's time to rest. A start-up routine might include preparing your materials, setting a timer, and taking three deep breaths. A shut-down routine could involve writing tomorrow's to-do list, filing away materials, and stretching.

By thoughtfully designing your environment, you make it easier to do the hard work of LSAT preparation and application writing. When focus becomes the default rather than something you have to fight for, you'll be amazed at what you can accomplish.

Here are some suggested books to check out to increase your focus.

"Indistractable: How to Control Your Attention and Choose Your Life" by Nir Eyal.

Indistractable is a practical guide that teaches you how to overcome distractions to achieve your goals and live a more focused, fulfilling life. This book helps while in pre-law, law school, and beyond.

"Grit: Why passion and resilience are the secrets to success" by Angela Duckworth

In this book, psychologist Angela Duckworth examines the qualities that contribute to achievement. "Grit" explores the role of perseverance and mindset in overcoming setbacks, suggesting these factors can be more important than talent or luck.

"Deep Work" by Cal Newport

Law school requires sustained, concentrated mental effort. Newport's strategies for developing the ability to focus without distraction will help you maximize your LSAT preparation and develop study habits that will serve you throughout law school.

"Atomic Habits" by James Clear

Success in the pre-law journey depends on consistent daily actions. Clear's system for building good habits and breaking bad ones provides practical strategies for creating the daily routines that lead to long-term success in law school and beyond.

"Make It Stick" by Peter C. Brown, Henry L. Roediger III, and Mark A. McDaniel

This research-based book on effective learning techniques will transform your study habits. Its evidence-based strategies for retention and comprehension will help you prepare more effectively for the LSAT and develop the learning skills needed for law school success.

"Getting Things Done" by David Allen

Law school and legal practice involve managing multiple competing priorities and deadlines. Allen's system for organizing tasks and projects will help you develop the organizational skills needed to juggle LSAT preparation, applications, coursework, and eventually, legal cases.

Chapter 4: Set the Foundation Early and Strategize

Strategic Course Selection

The courses you take as an undergraduate can significantly impact your law school readiness, yet many students don't think strategically about their class choices until it's too late. While there's no "pre-law major" requirement, certain courses can help you develop essential skills, boost your GPA, and demonstrate your readiness for legal education.

If you have already completed your undergraduate degree, and feel like you could use a boost, consider a master's degree to provide additional evidence of your academic strengths.

First, understand what law schools value in your academic background:

- Strong analytical and critical thinking skills
- Excellent reading comprehension and writing abilities
- Logical reasoning capabilities
- Research proficiency
- Public speaking and argumentation skills
- Intense scholarly reading and writing skills

With these priorities in mind, consider including these types of courses in your undergraduate plan:

Skill-Building Courses:

- Logic and critical thinking classes (often found in philosophy departments)

- Research-intensive courses that require substantial writing
- Public speaking, debate, or argumentation classes
- Advanced composition or rhetoric courses
- Statistics or research methods (helpful for understanding empirical legal studies)

Content-Relevant Courses:

- Constitutional history
- Political science courses on government and law
- Business law or ethics classes
- Courses examining social justice issues
- International relations or comparative political systems

When evaluating potential courses, look beyond just the subject matter. Consider:

The Professor: Research professors before registering. Look for instructors known for:

- Clear expectations and fair grading
- Strong feedback on writing
- Teaching style that matches your learning preferences
- Willingness to mentor students and write recommendations

The Assessment Methods: Courses that evaluate you through research papers, presentations, and analytical assignments often better prepare you for law school than those relying solely on multiple-choice exams.

The Workload Balance: Plan each semester with a mix of more and less demanding courses. Taking four writing-intensive classes simultaneously might tank your GPA, while a balanced schedule allows you to excel in each course.

Remember that your GPA matters significantly in law school admissions. Sometimes the strategic choice is to take the interesting but challenging course pass/fail while focusing your graded efforts on classes where you're likely to excel.

Consider Amir's approach: As a political science major, he balanced each semester with two courses in his major, one challenging "skill builder" (like formal logic or advanced research methods), one GPA-friendly elective in subjects he excelled in, and one exploration course in areas that genuinely interested him. This strategy allowed him to maintain a strong GPA while developing the skills law schools value.

Don't wait until junior year to think strategically. From your very first semester, approach course selection with your law school goals in mind. This doesn't mean avoiding challenging courses, it means choosing challenges that build relevant skills while maintaining the strong GPA you'll need for competitive applications.

Building Recommender Relationships

STRONG RECOMMENDATION letters can transform a good application into a great one. Yet many students make a critical mistake: they wait until application season to start building relationships with potential recommenders. By then, it's often too late to develop the meaningful connections that lead to compelling, personal letters.

The best recommendation letters come from people who know you well, not just as a name on a class roster, but as a student with unique qualities, work ethic, and potential. Building these relationships takes time and intentionality.

Start identifying potential recommenders early, ideally by sophomore year. Look for:

- Professors who teach smaller, discussion-based classes.
- Instructors in your major or in pre-law relevant subjects.
- Faculty advisors for clubs or activities you're involved in.
- Supervisors from internships or work experiences.
- Mentors from volunteer or community service work.

Once you've identified potential recommenders, focus on building genuine relationships:

In Academic Settings:

- Participate actively in class discussions.
- Visit office hours regularly—not just when you need help.
- Ask thoughtful questions that demonstrate your engagement.
- Follow up on interesting discussion points via email.
- Request feedback on papers or projects and implement suggestions.
- Share relevant articles or ideas that connect to class topics.

In Work or Volunteer Settings:

- Take initiative beyond your assigned tasks.
- Ask for feedback and act on it.
- Express interest in your supervisor's career path.
- Request additional responsibilities that showcase your abilities.
- Document your accomplishments and contributions.

The key is consistency. Brief, regular interactions over time create a much stronger impression than a single memorable conversation.

Create a system to track your relationship-building efforts. Keep notes on:

- Which professors' office hours you've attended.
- Topics discussed during these meetings.
- Feedback received and how you implemented it.
- Special projects or additional work you've done.
- Personal connections made (shared interests, memorable conversations).

This information will be invaluable when you later ask for recommendations, as you can remind recommenders of specific interactions and accomplishments.

Timing matters too. Aim to have solid relationships with at least three potential recommenders by the end of your junior year. This gives you options when application time arrives and ensures you're not scrambling for last-minute letters.

Consider Elena's approach: From her freshman year, she identified one professor each semester to connect with beyond classroom requirements. She visited office hours at least three times per term, participated actively in class, and occasionally shared articles relevant to course topics. By junior year, she had five professors who knew her well enough to write strong recommendations, giving her options when application time arrived.

Remember that building these relationships isn't just about securing recommendations, it's about creating a network of mentors who can guide your academic and professional development. The professors who write your law school recommendations may later become valuable connections as you navigate your legal career.

Here are sample letters you can use to request a recommendation.

Subject: Materials for Law School Recommendation Letter

Dear Professor [Name],

Thank you for agreeing to write a letter of recommendation for my law school applications. I truly appreciate your support of my legal education goals.

As promised, I've attached the following materials to assist you:

My current resume highlighting my academic and extracurricular achievements

A draft of my personal statement discussing [brief description of content]

A list of the courses I've taken with you, including grades and notable assignments

A document outlining my law school goals and the specific qualities I hope you might address

For your reference, I am applying to the following schools with these deadlines:

All recommendations should be submitted through the LSAC system. You should receive an email from LSAC with submission instructions within the next few days.

Please let me know if you need any additional information. I'm happy to meet in person to discuss my goals further if that would be helpful.

Thank you again for your support.

Sincerely,

[Your Full Name]

[University] Class of [Year]

[Phone Number]

[Email Address]

Subject: Friendly Reminder: Recommendation Letter for Law School
Dear Professor [Name],

I hope this email finds you well. I'm writing to check in regarding the letter of recommendation for my law school applications that you kindly agreed to write.

My first application deadline is approaching on [specific date], and LSAC recommends having all materials submitted at least two weeks in advance. If you've already submitted your letter, please accept my sincere thanks and disregard this reminder.

Please let me know if you need any additional information from me to complete the letter. I'm happy to provide whatever would be helpful.

Thank you again for your support of my law school aspirations. I greatly appreciate your time and guidance.

Best regards,
[Your Full Name]
[University] Class of [Year]
[Phone Number]
[Email Address]

GPA Management

YOUR UNDERGRADUATE GPA is one of the most important factors in law school admissions—and unlike your LSAT score, it can't be changed with a few months of intensive study. From your very first semester, every grade matters.

Law schools look at your GPA in several ways:

- Your cumulative GPA across all courses.
- Your "major GPA" in your primary field of study
- Grade trends over time (improving grades look better than declining ones).
- The rigor of your course selection.

They also consider these numbers in context of your school's reputation and grading policies. A 3.7 at a school known for grade inflation might be viewed differently than the same GPA at an institution with rigorous standards.

Here's how to manage your GPA strategically from day one:

Start strong. Many students underestimate freshman courses, thinking they'll be easy. This mistake can create a GPA hole that's difficult to climb out of. Treat every course seriously from the beginning.

Know your strengths. Be honest about your academic strengths and weaknesses. If quantitative reasoning isn't your strong suit, balance any required math or science courses with subjects where you excel.

Understand grading policies. Some schools offer grade forgiveness for retaken courses, while others average both attempts. Know your school's policies for withdrawals, pass/fail options, and grade replacement.

Monitor your progress. Don't wait for midterms to realize you're struggling. Check in with yourself weekly: Are you understanding the material? Completing assignments thoroughly? Preparing adequately for assessments?

Develop effective study strategies. Different courses require different approaches:

- For memorization-heavy courses: Use spaced repetition and active recall techniques.
- For problem-solving courses: Practice with varied examples and explain concepts in your own words.
- For writing-intensive courses: Start assignments early and build in time for revisions.

Create grade recovery plans. If you receive a disappointing grade on an assignment or exam:

- Analyze what went wrong (misunderstanding concepts, poor time management, test anxiety?).
- Meet with your professor to discuss improvement strategies.
- Adjust your study approach for the next assessment.
- Calculate what grades you'll need on remaining assignments to achieve your target.

Use campus resources. Most colleges offer free tutoring, writing centers, academic coaching, and study groups. Using these resources isn't a sign of weakness, it's a strategy employed by successful students.

Consider Tomas, who received a C on his first college paper. Instead of panicking, he visited his professor's office hours to understand his mistakes, then took his next draft to the writing center before submission. He earned an A- on the next paper and ended the course with a B+, protecting his cumulative GPA.

If you do experience a difficult semester due to personal circumstances, health issues, or other challenges, document everything. You may need to explain grade dips in an addendum to your law school applications.

The goal isn't perfection—it's excellence within your capabilities. A thoughtful, strategic approach to GPA management from day one will give you a strong foundation for competitive law school applications.

Get Your Money Right

LAW SCHOOL IS EXPENSIVE, plain and simple; it's crucial to get a handle on your finances early so money doesn't become a barrier to your legal dreams. Understanding the costs involved and developing a smart financial strategy are key components of your pre-law BE§T MODE.

First, let's break down the real costs. Tuition is the big one, obviously. But don't forget living expenses: rent, food, transportation, books, and those unexpected costs that always seem to pop up. Law school costs vary ridiculously depending on location and whether it's public or private. A state school in a smaller town will be much cheaper than a private university in New York City or Los Angeles.

Start researching the cost of living in cities where you're considering applying. Websites like Numbeo and Expatistan can help you compare the cost of everything from a loaf of bread to apartment rentals across different cities. Also, look at the specific law schools' websites. They usually have a cost of attendance breakdown that includes tuition, fees, and estimated living expenses.

For example, let's say you are considering schools in both Austin, Texas, and Boston, Massachusetts. Living in Boston is notoriously expensive, especially when it comes to housing. You'll need to factor in potentially double the rent compared to Austin. Public transportation in Boston is good, but you might still need a car, adding to the expense. Austin, while growing in cost, offers more affordable housing options outside the city center and has lower transportation costs overall. Being aware of these differences early on lets you make informed decisions about where to apply and, ultimately, where to attend.

Okay, you know the costs. Now, how are you going to pay for it? This is where financial aid comes in. Financial aid can come from many sources, including the government (federal loans), the law school itself (scholarships and grants), and outside organizations (private scholarships). Start with the Free Application for Federal Student Aid (FAFSA). This form determines your eligibility for federal student loans, including Direct Stafford Loans and Grad PLUS Loans (to the extent that they are still available). The FAFSA opens every year in October, and you should fill it out as soon as possible because some aid is awarded on a first-come, first-served basis.

As of the time of this publication, Direct Stafford Loans come in two forms: subsidized and unsubsidized. Subsidized loans, available to students with demonstrated financial need, don't accrue interest while you're in school. Unsubsidized loans, available to all eligible students regardless of need, start accruing interest as soon as they're disbursed. Grad PLUS Loans are available to graduate students and allow you to borrow up to the total cost of attendance, minus any other financial aid you receive. However, Grad PLUS Loans typically have higher interest rates than Stafford Loans, so exhaust those options first.

Next, investigate the financial aid options offered directly by the law schools you're interested in. Many schools offer merit-based scholarships based on your LSAT score and GPA. Some also offer need-based grants to students with demonstrated financial need. Check each school's website for details on their financial aid programs and application procedures. Pay close attention to deadlines, as these can be different from the general application deadlines.

Don't stop there. Cast a wide net for external scholarships. There are tons of organizations that offer scholarships to law students, based on everything from academic achievement to community involvement to specific areas of interest. Start with online scholarship databases like Sallie Mae, AccessLex and Scholarship America. Filter your search based on your background, interests, and academic profile to find scholarships you're eligible for.

Also, look for scholarships offered by bar associations, law firms, and other legal organizations. These scholarships often have a connection to the legal profession, which can make you a more attractive candidate. For example, if you're interested in environmental law, look for scholarships offered by environmental law organizations. If you're a member of a minority group, explore scholarships offered by minority bar associations.

When applying for scholarships, pay attention to the application requirements. Most scholarships require you to submit an essay, transcripts, letters of recommendation, and a resume. Tailor your application to each scholarship, highlighting your qualifications and explaining why you're a good fit for the award. Proofread everything carefully before submitting, and make sure to meet the deadline.

Beyond loans and scholarships, think about how you can minimize your expenses while in law school. One option is to live with roommates to split the cost of rent and utilities. Another is to cook your own meals instead of eating out all the time. Look for discounts on textbooks and other school supplies. Many law schools have used book sales or online forums where students can buy and sell used books.

Also, consider working part-time during law school to help offset your expenses. Many law students work as research assistants, tutors, or interns at law firms or legal organizations. However, be careful not to overcommit yourself. Law school is demanding, and you need to prioritize your studies.

Okay, so all of the above is for during law school, but this is pre-law. How does this all relate? Well, getting your finances in order BEFORE you start law school is just as important. If you start law school with existing debt, that will add to the financial burden you will face. Any steps you can take to minimize debt before law school will pay off well in the long run.

That means now is the time to buckle down on saving. Create a budget and track your spending to identify areas where you can cut back. Set a savings goal and make regular contributions to a savings account. Even small amounts can add up over time. Consider a side hustle to earn extra income. There are tons of online opportunities to make money, such as freelancing, tutoring, or selling products on Etsy.

Think about your credit score. Your credit score impacts the interest rates you'll receive on student loans. The higher your score, the lower your interest rate, which can save you thousands of dollars over the life of the loan. Check your credit report regularly and take steps to improve your score if necessary. Pay your bills on time, keep your credit card balances low, and avoid opening too many new accounts at once.

Finally, let's talk about planning for bar prep. The bar exam is the final hurdle to becoming a lawyer, and it's notoriously expensive to prepare for. Bar prep courses can cost several thousand dollars, and you'll also need to factor in the cost of study materials, application fees, and living expenses during the study period. Start saving for bar prep now, even if it seems far off. Set aside a small amount each month and put it in a dedicated savings account. Look for discounts on bar prep courses. Many companies offer early bird discounts or discounts to students who meet certain criteria. Also, explore bar prep loan options. Some lenders offer loans specifically for bar prep expenses.

For example, let's consider the cost of a typical bar prep course, say $3,000. If you start saving $100 per month three years before you graduate from law school, you'll have accumulated $3,600, more than enough to cover the course fees. Add in potential discounts or financial assistance, and you'll significantly reduce the financial stress associated with bar prep.

Getting your finances right before law school is an investment in your future. It's about more than just paying the bills. It's about setting yourself up for success and giving yourself the freedom to pursue your legal dreams without being weighed down by financial stress. By understanding the costs, exploring financial aid options, managing your spending, and saving early and often, you can achieve your goal of becoming a lawyer.

Chapter 5: Train for the LSAT

LSAT Section Overview

The LSAT often feels like a mysterious beast to pre-law students. Let's demystify it by breaking down exactly what you'll face on test day.

As of August 2024, the LSAT has officially changed its format. The test now consists of four sections, but only three count toward your score. Here's the breakdown:

Logical Reasoning (LR) – Two Sections

Logical Reasoning is now the star of the LSAT show, making up half of your scored test. You'll get two LR sections, and they test your ability to analyze, evaluate, and complete arguments.

Expect short passages with questions asking you to:

- Identify the main conclusion of an argument
- Spot the assumptions an argument is built on Strengthen or weaken reasoning
- Recognize logical flaws
- Draw proper inferences

Think of this as the "argument section" of the test. The LSAT is checking if you can see the bones of an argument, take it apart, and put it back together. These skills mirror what you'll do every day in law school—reading cases, debating positions, and writing persuasive arguments.

Reading Comprehension (RC) – One Section

This section gives you four passages (sometimes including a set of two shorter, related texts for a "comparative reading" exercise). Each passage is followed by 5–8 questions.

Here you'll need to:

- Pinpoint the main idea and author's purpose
- Understand how the passage is structured
- Make inferences beyond what's explicitly stated
- Apply principles to new contexts

RC isn't about speed-reading, it's about wrestling with dense, complex material, the same way you'll be parsing statutes, judicial opinions, and legal commentary in law school.

Writing Sample – Unscored but Required

Finally, you'll face the unscored Writing Sample. You'll be asked to write an essay choosing between two positions and backing up your choice with reasoning. Law schools can review this as part of your application, so it's worth taking seriously, even though it won't affect your score.

Key Details to Know

Scoring: The LSAT is scored on a 120–180 scale, with the median hovering around 151. Top-tier schools are usually looking for scores in the 160s and 170s.

Timing: Each section is 35 minutes, which translates to about 1.5 minutes per question in Logical Reasoning, and a tight squeeze in Reading Comprehension.

Purpose: The LSAT doesn't test legal knowledge. It tests the skills that predict law school success: careful reading, logical analysis, and argument evaluation. And yes—these are skills you can sharpen with consistent practice.

WHY THIS MATTERS

The removal of the old "Logic Games" section was a major shift. Now, your performance hinges even more on your ability to break down arguments and engage with complex texts. The good news? These skills are directly transferable to law school and beyond.

Understanding this new structure is your first step toward building a smart prep plan. Instead of just grinding through random practice questions, you can train with purpose—strengthening the exact skills that will carry you not just through the LSAT, but through law school itself.

Standardized Test Mindset

THE LSAT ISN'T JUST a test of logical reasoning and reading comprehension—it's a mental game. Your mindset can be the difference between underperforming and reaching your full potential.

Many students with strong academic records struggle with standardized tests because they approach them with counterproductive mindsets. Let's transform your thinking to set yourself up for success:

Embrace the Process, Not Just the Outcome

Instead of fixating solely on your target score, focus on the process of improvement. Each practice session is building neural pathways that strengthen your testing abilities. Track your progress in specific question types or skills rather than obsessing over your overall score.

Reframe Anxiety as Excitement

The physical symptoms of anxiety (increased heart rate, heightened alertness) are nearly identical to excitement. Before practice tests, try saying "I'm excited to see what I can do" rather than "I'm so nervous." This simple reframing can transform nervous energy into performance-enhancing focus.

Develop a Growth Mindset for the LSAT

Believe that your LSAT abilities can improve with effort and strategy. When you miss a question, think "I haven't mastered this yet" rather than "I'm not good at this." This mindset shift keeps you resilient through the inevitable challenges of preparation.

Create Performance Rituals

Olympic athletes use pre-performance rituals to enter their optimal state—you should too. Develop a consistent routine for the day before and morning of practice tests: what you eat, what you wear, how you warm up your brain. By test day, these rituals will trigger your test-taking state automatically.

Practice Stress Management Techniques

Learn and regularly practice techniques that help you manage test anxiety:

- Box breathing (inhale for 4 counts, hold for 4, exhale for 4, hold for 4)
- Progressive muscle relaxation (tensing and releasing muscle groups)
- Visualization of successful test performance
- Positive self-talk and affirmations specific to test-taking

Build Mental Stamina

The LSAT is a mental marathon. Gradually build your concentration endurance by increasing the length of your focused study sessions. Work up to completing full practice tests under timed conditions without breaks.

Develop a Relationship with the Test

Rather than viewing the LSAT as your enemy, see it as a challenging but fair assessment that rewards preparation. Some students even name their test ("I'm going to show Terry the LSAT what I've learned today") to create a less adversarial relationship.

Consider Jamal, who struggled with severe test anxiety despite knowing the material. He implemented a pre-test ritual of five minutes of box breathing followed by reviewing his "greatest hits"—a list of challenging questions he had mastered. This routine helped him enter each practice session with confidence rather than dread. Over time, his practice scores improved by several points.

The mindset work isn't separate from your LSAT preparation, it's an integral part of it. Schedule regular time to practice these psychological approaches alongside your content review and practice questions.

By training your mind alongside your logical reasoning skills, you'll approach test day with the confidence and mental tools to perform at your best.

LSAT Resource Guide

WITH COUNTLESS LSAT preparation options available, finding the right resources for your learning style and budget can feel overwhelming. This guide will help you navigate the landscape of LSAT prep materials and create a personalized study plan.

Essential Free Resources

LSAC Official Materials:

- LSAC's free Khan Academy partnership offers personalized practice
- The Official LSAT Prep app provides one free practice test
- LSAC's website offers sample questions and test-taking tips
- Community Resources:
- r/LSAT on Reddit has valuable discussion threads and study groups
- 7Sage's free Logic Games explanations on YouTube
- The Thinking LSAT podcast offers strategy advice and question analysis

Recommended Paid Resources

Self-Study Books:

- The LSAT Trainer by Mike Kim ($60) - Excellent for beginners
- PowerScore LSAT Bible Trilogy ($200) - Comprehensive coverage of all sections
- The Loophole in Logical Reasoning by Ellen Cassidy ($40) - Game-changing approach to LR
- LSAT Prep Books by Manhattan Prep ($75) - Clear explanations and strategies
- Practice Tests:
- 10 Actual, Official LSAT PrepTests series ($30 per volume) - Essential for realistic practice
- LSAC's Official LSAT Prep Plus subscription ($99/year) - Access to 70+ official practice tests
- Courses:
- 7Sage ($69/month) - Comprehensive curriculum with analytics

- Blueprint ($249-$1,699) - Engaging video lessons and personalized study plans
- PowerScore ($395-$1,595) - Structured curriculum with proven methods
- Princeton Review ($799-$1,599) - Traditional approach with guaranteed score improvement
- TestMasters ($1,150-$1,850) - Rigorous curriculum with extensive practice

Tutoring:

- Private tutors ($80-$200/hour) - Personalized guidance and accountability
- Group tutoring ($40-$80/hour) - More affordable option for personalized help

How to Choose What's Right for You
Consider these factors when selecting resources:
Learning Style:

- Visual learners may prefer video-based courses like 7Sage or Blueprint
- Reading-oriented learners might do well with books like the PowerScore Bibles
- Interactive learners should look for platforms with practice drills and feedback

Budget Constraints:

- Limited budget: Start with free Khan Academy and add The LSAT Trainer
- Moderate budget: Self-study books + Official PrepTests + a month of an online course
- Larger budget: Comprehensive course or tutoring + all official practice materials

Time Available:

- 6+ months: Self-paced options like books and flexible online courses
- 3-6 months: Structured courses with set schedules
- Under 3 months: Intensive courses or focused tutoring

Starting Point:

- Complete beginners benefit from comprehensive courses
- Those with some familiarity might need targeted help in specific sections
- Students who've taken the test before should focus on personalized analysis of weaknesses

Remember that more expensive doesn't always mean better results. Many students achieve their target scores through disciplined self-study with books and official practice tests.

The most important resource is official LSAT questions. Whatever approach you choose, ensure you're practicing with real LSAT questions, not imitations.

- Create a balanced study plan that includes:
- Learning the core concepts and strategies
- Practicing with individual questions by type
- Taking full, timed practice tests
- Reviewing your mistakes thoroughly
- Addressing test anxiety and mindset

By thoughtfully selecting resources that match your learning style, budget, and needs, you'll create an effective LSAT preparation plan that maximizes your score improvement.

LSAT Study Timeline

PREPARING FOR THE LSAT isn't a sprint—it's a marathon that requires careful pacing. Starting too late leads to cramming and anxiety, while an overly long study period can cause burnout. This timeline will help you plan your LSAT journey strategically.

12+ Months Before Target Test Date: Exploration Phase

- Take a diagnostic test to establish your baseline
- Familiarize yourself with the test format and question types
- Begin building logical thinking skills through puzzles and reading
- Research preparation methods and resources
- Set a target score based on your law school goals
- Create a realistic study schedule based on your other commitments

9-12 Months Before: Foundation Building

- Study core concepts for each section (2-3 hours, 2-3 times per week)
- Learn the fundamental strategies for approaching each question type
- Begin untimed practice with individual questions
- Develop a system for tracking your progress and identifying weaknesses
- Build study habits that you can sustain long-term
- Take a practice test every 4-6 weeks to gauge progress

6-9 Months Before: Skill Development

- Increase study time to 8-10 hours per week
- Practice timed sections regularly
- Focus on your weakest areas while maintaining strengths
- Begin implementing test-day strategies (guessing strategy, time management)
- Take a practice test every 3-4 weeks
- Refine your study methods based on what's working

3-6 Months Before: Intensive Practice

- Ramp up to 12-15 hours of study per week
- Complete timed practice tests every 2 weeks
- Analyze mistakes thoroughly and create targeted drills
- Practice with the most recent LSAT questions available
- Begin simulating test-day conditions (same time of day, full test in one sitting)
- Address test anxiety with mindfulness and stress-reduction techniques

1-3 Months Before: Peak Performance

- Study 15-20 hours per week
- Take weekly full-length practice tests under strict test-day conditions
- Focus on fine-tuning your approach and eliminating careless errors
- Review your performance analytics to address any remaining weaknesses
- Practice your test-day routine (sleep schedule, meals, transportation)
- Register for your test date if you haven't already

Final Month: Refinement and Readiness

- Maintain consistent practice without overexertion
- Continue weekly practice tests through the second-to-last weekend
- Review your notes on common mistakes and key strategies
- Finalize your test-day plan (timing strategy, break routine, etc.)
- Taper your studying in the final week to prevent burnout
- Focus on mental preparation and confidence building

Sample Weekly Schedules
Early Phase (9-12 months out):

- Monday: 1 hour concept review
- Wednesday: 1.5 hours practice questions
- Saturday: 2 hours section practice

- Monthly: Full practice test and review
- Middle Phase (3-6 months out):
- Monday: 2 hours logical reasoning practice
- Tuesday: 1.5 hours reading comprehension
- Thursday: 2 hours analytical reasoning
- Saturday: 3.5 hours practice test
- Sunday: 3 hours test review and weakness drilling
- Final Phase (1-3 months out):
- Monday: 2 hours weakness drilling
- Tuesday: 3 hours timed section practice
- Wednesday: 2 hours review and strategy refinement
- Thursday: 2 hours weakness drilling
- Saturday: 4 hours full practice test
- Sunday: 3 hours thorough test review

Remember that consistency trumps intensity. Studying for one hour daily is more effective than cramming for seven hours once a week.

Adjust this timeline based on your starting point and target score. If your diagnostic is already close to your goal, you might need less time. If you're aiming for a substantial increase, you might need the full 12 months or more.

By planning your LSAT preparation thoughtfully and giving yourself adequate time, you'll approach test day with confidence and the skills needed to achieve your best possible score.

Chapter 6: Master Your Mindset

Emotional Fitness Training

Just as physical fitness prepares your body for athletic challenges, emotional fitness prepares your mind for the psychological demands of the pre-law journey. The LSAT, application process, and waiting for decisions can trigger stress, self-doubt, and anxiety—unless you've built your emotional muscles in advance.

Emotional fitness isn't about eliminating negative feelings, it's about developing the capacity to experience difficult emotions without being derailed by them. Here's how to build your emotional resilience:

Develop Stress Awareness

Before you can manage stress, you need to recognize its early warning signs:

- Physical signals (tension headaches, disrupted sleep, stomach issues)
- Emotional indicators (irritability, anxiety, mood swings)
- Behavioral changes (procrastination, isolation, comfort eating)

Create a personal stress inventory by tracking these signals for two weeks. Note what triggers them and how they affect your productivity and wellbeing.

Build Your Stress Management Toolkit

Different stress management techniques work for different people and situations. Experiment with these approaches to build your personal toolkit:

- Quick Reset Techniques (1-5 minutes):
- Box breathing or 4-7-8 breathing
- Progressive muscle relaxation

- Sensory grounding (identify 5 things you can see, 4 you can touch, 3 you can hear, 2 you can smell, 1 you can taste)
- Brief mindfulness meditation
- Physical movement (jumping jacks, stretching)
- Daily Practices (10-30 minutes):
- Journaling about emotions and challenges
- Meditation or yoga
- Physical exercise
- Time in nature
- Creative expression (art, music, writing)
- Weekly Restoration (1-3 hours):
- Complete digital detox
- Social connection with supportive friends
- Engaging in hobbies unrelated to law
- Volunteering or helping others
- Spiritual or religious practices

Practice Emotional Regulation

Law school preparation will trigger strong emotions. Learn to:

Name your emotions specifically. "I'm feeling disappointed about my practice test score" is more manageable than "I feel terrible."

Accept emotions without judgment. Instead of "I shouldn't be anxious about this," try "I notice I'm feeling anxious right now, and that's okay."

Respond rather than react. Create space between feeling and action by pausing to ask, "What would be most helpful right now?"

Practice self-compassion. Speak to yourself as you would to a good friend facing the same challenge.

Build Resilience Through Controlled Challenges

Deliberately expose yourself to manageable discomfort to build resilience:

- Take a practice test under slightly challenging conditions
- Seek constructive criticism on your personal statement
- Try a new activity where you'll initially struggle
- Speak up in classes even when you're uncertain

After each challenge, reflect: What emotions arose? How did you handle them? What would you do differently next time?

Consider Alicia, who panicked during her first practice LSAT. She developed a three-step emotional regulation routine: 1) Recognize and name her anxiety, 2) Take three deep breaths while reminding herself "This feeling is temporary," 3) Refocus on the immediate next step. By practicing this routine during study sessions, it became automatic during her actual LSAT, helping her stay calm and focused.

Emotional fitness training isn't separate from your pre-law preparation—it's an essential component that will serve you throughout your legal career. The lawyers who thrive aren't necessarily those with the highest LSAT scores, but those who can maintain their emotional balance under pressure.

Overcoming Mental Obstacles

THE PATH TO LAW SCHOOL is as much a mental challenge as an academic one. Even the most qualified candidates face psychological barriers that can derail their progress if not addressed. Let's tackle the most common mental obstacles head-on:

Fear of Failure

Fear of failure can paralyze your preparation or lead to self-sabotage. Signs include procrastination, perfectionism, or avoiding challenges altogether.

Strategies to overcome:

- Redefine failure as feedback rather than a final judgment
- Set process goals (study hours, questions completed) alongside outcome goals (target scores)
- Create a "failure resume" listing setbacks you've overcome to remind yourself of your resilience
- Visualize recovering from disappointment rather than just visualizing success

Imposter Syndrome

Many pre-law students secretly worry they're not "law school material" despite evidence to the contrary. This belief can undermine confidence and performance.

Strategies to overcome:

- Collect and review positive feedback and accomplishments
- Recognize that feeling uncertain doesn't mean you're unqualified
- Connect with other pre-law students to normalize these feelings
- Focus on growth rather than fixed abilities
- Remember that many successful attorneys once felt exactly as you do

Comparison Trap

Constantly measuring yourself against peers can create anxiety and distort your self-perception.

Strategies to overcome:

- Limit exposure to forums and social media where comparison thrives.
- Track your progress against your own baseline, not others'.
- Remember that people share successes more readily than struggles.
- Use others' achievements as information and inspiration, not judgment.
- Focus on your unique strengths and perspective.

Perfectionism

The pursuit of flawlessness often leads to procrastination, excessive stress, and diminishing returns on effort.

Strategies to overcome:

Adopt the "85% rule"—aim for 85% perfect, then move forward

- Set time limits for tasks to prevent endless revisions.
- Practice deliberate imperfection in low-stakes situations.
- Focus on progress and improvement rather than perfection.
- Remember that perfect LSAT scores and flawless applications are rare.

Catastrophic Thinking

The tendency to imagine worst-case scenarios ("If I don't get into my top choice, my career is over") creates unnecessary anxiety.

Strategies to overcome:

- Challenge catastrophic thoughts with evidence and alternatives.
- Use the "and then what?" technique to follow feared outcomes to their logical conclusion.
- Develop contingency plans to reduce uncertainty.
- Practice bringing your focus back to the present moment.

Remember that many successful lawyers faced setbacks in their education journey

Practical Techniques for Daily Use

Thought Records: When negative thoughts arise, write down:

- The situation that triggered the thought.
- The automatic thought that occurred.
- Evidence that supports and contradicts the thought.
- A more balanced alternative thought.

Mental Contrasting: Visualize your goal, then identify obstacles, then plan how to overcome each obstacle.

Cognitive Defusion: Create distance from unhelpful thoughts by:

- Prefacing thoughts with "I'm having the thought that..."
- Saying thoughts in a silly voice
- Thanking your mind for the thought and refocusing on your task

Values Alignment: When motivation wanes, reconnect with how your current tasks align with your core values and long-term goals.

Consider David, who struggled with perfectionism that led him to spend way too much time on a single LSAT question. He implemented a timer system that forced him to move on after a set time and kept a "good enough" journal where he recorded instances when his "good enough" efforts yielded positive results. Over time, he learned that perfectionism was actually hindering his progress rather than helping it.

By recognizing and actively addressing these mental obstacles, you transform them from roadblocks into opportunities for growth—developing psychological skills that will serve you throughout your legal career.

Self Compassion Practices

THE JOURNEY TO LAW school can be brutally demanding. In a culture that often glorifies hustle and sacrifice, it's easy to become your own harshest critic. Yet research consistently shows that self-compassion—not self-criticism—leads to greater resilience, motivation, and achievement.

Self-compassion isn't self-indulgence or lowering your standards. It's treating yourself with the same kindness and understanding you would offer a good friend facing similar challenges. Here's how to practice self-compassion throughout your pre-law journey.

You Are Not Behind: A Reality Check

One of the most common sources of pre-law anxiety is the feeling that you're "behind" where you should be. This feeling is almost always distorted.

When these thoughts arise, try this pep talk:

"There is no single timeline for becoming a lawyer. Some of the most successful attorneys started law school in their 30s, 40s, or beyond. Each detour in my path has given me unique perspectives and experiences that will enrich my legal practice. My journey isn't behind schedule—it's exactly where it needs to be right now.

The legal profession needs diverse perspectives and life experiences. My unique path isn't a liability—it's an asset that will help me connect with clients and approach legal problems in distinctive ways.

Right now, I'm exactly where I need to be, taking the next right step on my own authentic path to becoming the lawyer I'm meant to be."

Mindfulness for Pre-Law Students

Mindfulness—the practice of present-moment awareness without judgment—is particularly valuable for pre-law students. It helps you recognize self-critical thoughts before they spiral and brings you back to the present when you're caught in worry about the future.

Try this simple 5-minute practice:

- Sit comfortably and close your eyes or lower your gaze
- Bring attention to your breath, noticing the sensation of breathing
- When your mind wanders to thoughts about law school, applications, or the future, gently note "thinking" and return to your breath
- If self-critical thoughts arise, note "criticism" and return to your breath
- Continue this practice for 5 minutes, gradually increasing the time as you become comfortable

Even 5 minutes daily builds the mental muscle to notice and disengage from unhelpful thought patterns.

Self-Compassion in Specific Pre-Law Scenarios

After a disappointing LSAT practice test:

"This score is difficult to see, and it's natural to feel disappointed. Many successful lawyers struggled with the LSAT at first. This score doesn't define my potential as a lawyer—it's information about what I need to focus on next. I'm going to take some time to feel this disappointment, then make a plan to address the areas where I can improve."

When comparing yourself to peers:

"It's human to compare myself to others, but everyone's journey is different. I don't know the full story behind others' achievements or struggles. The only productive comparison is between where I am today and where I was yesterday. I'm going to refocus on my own progress and celebrate the steps I've taken."

When feeling overwhelmed by the application process:

"This process is designed to be challenging, and feeling overwhelmed is a normal response. I don't need to figure everything out at once. Today, I'll focus on just one small step. Taking care of my wellbeing isn't a distraction from my goals—it's essential to achieving them."

Daily Self-Compassion Practices

Morning self-compassion check-in: Before checking emails or social media, place a hand on your heart and ask, *"How am I feeling today? What do I need to support myself?"*

Compassionate goal setting: When planning your day, ask not just "What do I want to accomplish?" but also "How can I be kind to myself in the process?"

Self-compassion breaks: When you notice stress or self-criticism during the day, pause for three deep breaths while mentally saying, *"This is a moment of difficulty. Difficulty is part of the pre-law journey. May I be kind to myself right now."*

Evening reflection: Before sleep, note three things you did well today (no matter how small) and one way you'll show yourself compassion tomorrow.

Consider Maya, who berated herself after scoring lower than expected on her first LSAT practice test. She began practicing self-compassion by writing a letter to herself from the perspective of a supportive friend. This shift in perspective helped her see that her harsh self-criticism wasn't motivating, it was paralyzing. By treating herself with more understanding, she actually studied more effectively and improved her score on subsequent tests.

Self-compassion isn't a detour from your law school goals, it's the foundation that will support you through the challenges ahead and help you arrive at your destination with your wellbeing intact.

Chapter 7: Open Doors Before Closing

Essential Pre-Law Programs

The most successful law school applicants don't wait for opportunities to find them—they actively seek out experiences that will strengthen their applications and prepare them for legal education. Pre-law programs and internships can provide valuable skills, connections, and credentials that set you apart from other applicants.

Summer Pre-Law Programs

Council on Legal Education Opportunity (CLEO):

Programs: College Scholars Program, Achieving Success in the Application Process (ASAP)

Benefits: LSAT preparation, application guidance, networking with law school admissions officers

Eligibility: Underrepresented students with strong academic potential

Deadlines: Applications typically due in February-March

Cost: Free or low-cost with scholarships available

SEO Law Fellowship:

Program: Paid summer internships at top law firms for pre-law students

Benefits: Real-world legal experience, mentorship, LSAT preparation

Eligibility: Rising seniors from underrepresented backgrounds with strong academic records

Deadlines: Applications open in August, due by December

Cost: Fellows receive stipends (approximately $1,000/week)

Summer Law School Prep Programs:

Many law schools offer summer programs for undergraduate students:

Columbia Law School's Summer Program for Undergraduates

Harvard Law School's Zero-L Program

Duke Law School's Pre-Law Fellowship

Benefits: Introduction to legal education, networking with faculty, strengthened applications

Deadlines: Typically January-March for summer programs

Cost: Varies ($1,500-$5,000, with scholarships often available)

Academic Year Opportunities

Ronald E. McNair Scholars Program:

Benefits: Research opportunities, graduate school preparation, mentorship

Eligibility: First-generation, low-income students and underrepresented groups

Deadlines: Varies by institution, typically early fall

Cost: Participants often receive stipends

Undergraduate Research Programs:

Look for research assistant positions with pre-law advisors or professors in political science, philosophy, or history departments

Benefits: Develops research skills, potential for publication, strong recommendation letters

How to apply: Approach professors directly with specific interest in their work

Timing: Start inquiring at the beginning of each semester

Campus Legal Clinics:

Many universities have legal aid clinics that accept undergraduate volunteers

Benefits: Direct exposure to legal practice, networking with law students and attorneys

How to apply: Contact your university's legal clinic or law school

Commitment: Typically 5-10 hours weekly during academic year

Internship Opportunities

Government Internships:

- Congressional internships (U.S. House and Senate offices)
- State legislature internships
- District Attorney or Public Defender offices

Benefits: Understanding of government and policy, networking, potential for recommendation letters

Application deadlines: Congressional internships typically due 3-4 months before start date

Compensation: Many are unpaid; look for scholarships or stipends through your university

Legal Non-Profit Internships:

- Legal Aid Societies
- American Civil Liberties Union (ACLU)
- Public Interest Legal Organizations

Benefits: Direct legal experience, exposure to public interest law, demonstrated commitment to service

Application timing: 3-6 months before desired start date

Compensation: Often unpaid; seek academic credit or university funding

Corporate Legal Department Internships:

Many large corporations offer undergraduate internships in their legal departments

Benefits: Exposure to corporate law, professional environment experience, often paid

Application deadlines: Typically September-November for summer positions

Compensation: Usually paid ($15-25/hour)

Maximizing Program Benefits

To get the most from these opportunities:

- Apply strategically: Target programs aligned with your specific legal interests and career goals
- Prepare thoroughly: Research the organization before interviews and demonstrate specific knowledge
- Document your experience: Keep a journal of projects, skills developed, and accomplishments
- Build relationships: Connect with supervisors and colleagues who can later serve as recommenders

- Reflect and articulate: Regularly consider how your experiences connect to your legal aspirations

Consider Sophia, who participated in her state's judicial internship program during her junior year. She maintained relationships with the judge and clerks, who not only wrote strong recommendation letters but also connected her with alumni at her target law schools. These connections gave her valuable insights for her applications and interviews.

By proactively seeking out these pre-law programs and internships, you're not just building your resume, you're gaining skills, connections, and experiences that will serve you throughout your legal education and career.

Pre-Law Networking Guide

NETWORKING MIGHT SOUND intimidating, but at its core, it's simply building professional relationships. For pre-law students, these connections can provide guidance, opportunities, and eventually, job prospects. The legal profession values relationships, and starting to build your network now will give you a significant advantage.

Pre-Law Societies and Organizations

Campus Pre-Law Society:

Benefits: Local events, peer support, campus-specific resources

How to maximize: Don't just attend meetings—volunteer for leadership positions

Commitment level: 2-4 hours monthly for general membership; more for leadership roles

Phi Alpha Delta (PAD) Pre-Law Fraternity:

Benefits: National network, LSAT prep resources, law school tours

Membership process: Application and dues (typically $100-150)

Commitment level: Varies by chapter, typically 3-5 hours monthly

Mock Trial and Moot Court Teams:

Benefits: Public speaking experience, legal reasoning practice, teamwork skills

Joining process: Usually requires tryouts or interviews

Commitment level: Substantial (5-10 hours weekly, more before competitions)

Tip: Even if you don't make the competitive team, many programs offer practice teams or class credit options

Undergraduate Law Review or Journal:

Benefits: Research, writing, and editing experience; published work for your resume

Joining process: Application or writing competition

Commitment level: 3-8 hours weekly

Tip: If your school doesn't have one, consider founding an undergraduate law journal

Making the Most of Membership

Simply joining organizations isn't enough—you need to engage actively:

- Attend consistently: Regular participation builds relationships and shows commitment
- Volunteer for visible roles: Organize events, manage social media, or coordinate speakers
- Connect one-on-one: Build individual relationships with officers and active members
- Propose initiatives: Identify gaps in programming and suggest solutions
- Document your contributions: Keep track of your roles and accomplishments for your resume

Building Your Professional Network

Beyond student organizations, develop connections with legal professionals:

Alumni Networks:

Start with your university's alumni database or LinkedIn alumni tool

Search for graduates practicing in your areas of interest

Approach with specific, brief requests for insight rather than general pleas for help

Sample outreach: "As a fellow [University] student interested in environmental law, I'd appreciate 15 minutes to learn about your career path"

Informational Interviews:

Prepare 5-7 thoughtful questions about their career path and advice

Keep to the scheduled time limit

Follow up with a thank-you note within 24 hours

Ask if they recommend anyone else you should speak with (this builds your network naturally)

Legal Community Events:

Bar association events (many have reduced student rates)

Court observations (most are open to the public)

Law school information sessions and workshops

Public lectures by legal scholars or judges

Approach these as learning opportunities first, networking second

Online Networking:

LinkedIn: Create a professional profile and join pre-law and legal interest groups

Twitter: Follow legal professionals, law schools, and legal organizations

Reddit: Participate thoughtfully in r/lawschooladmissions and r/prelaw communities

Remember that your online presence is visible to future employers and admissions committees

Networking for Introverts

If networking feels draining or inauthentic:

- Start with structured situations: Formal events with clear purposes are often easier than open-ended networking
- Prepare talking points: Having 2-3 questions ready reduces anxiety about conversation lulls
- Set manageable goals: Aim to have one quality conversation rather than meeting everyone in the room
- Use your listening skills: Introverts often excel at asking thoughtful questions and remembering details
- Schedule recovery time: Plan quiet time after networking events to recharge

Consider Taylor, who was naturally shy but joined her campus pre-law society. She volunteered to manage their social media, which allowed her to connect with speakers and alumni online before meeting them in person. This "warm introduction" approach made in-person networking less intimidating, and she eventually became the society's president, developing valuable leadership skills and connections.

Effective networking isn't about collecting business cards or LinkedIn connections—it's about building genuine relationships based on mutual interest and respect. Start small, be consistent, and focus on quality over quantity. The network you build now will support you throughout your legal education and career.

Here's a sample email you can use to do outreach.

Subject: Pre-Law Student Seeking Advice on Environmental Law Career

Dear [Attorney Name],

I am a [year] at [University] pursuing a pre-law track with a focus on [relevant major/minor]. I discovered your work through [how you found them - article, firm website, LinkedIn, etc.], and your experience in [specific area of law] aligns closely with my professional interests.

Would you be willing to meet for 20-30 minutes, either virtually or at your office, to discuss your career path and any advice for someone interested in [specific area of law]? I'm particularly interested in learning about [1-2 specific questions or topics].

I understand you have a demanding schedule, and I would be grateful for any time you could offer. I'm available [provide 2-3 specific time ranges] in the coming weeks and can accommodate your preferences.

Thank you for considering my request.

Sincerely,

[Your Full Name]

[University] Class of [Year]

[Phone Number]

[Email Address]

[LinkedIn profile link - optional]

Here's a sample follow up email.

Subject: Following Up: Pre-Law Student Seeking Advice

Dear [Attorney Name],

I'm following up on my email from [date] regarding the possibility of a brief conversation about your experience in [specific area of law]. I understand you have a busy schedule, so I wanted to reiterate my interest and flexibility.

I would value even 15 minutes of your time, either in person or by phone. If meeting isn't possible, I would be grateful for any written advice you might share about entering the [specific] field of law.

Thank you for considering my request.

Best regards,

[Your Full Name]

[University] Class of [Year]

[Phone Number]

[Email Address]

Here's a sample thank you email.

Subject: Thank You for Your Time and Insights

Dear [Attorney Name],

Thank you for taking the time to speak with me yesterday about your experience in [specific area of law]. Your insights about [specific topic discussed] were particularly helpful, and I appreciate your suggestion to [specific advice they gave].

I've already [action you've taken based on their advice], and I plan to explore the resources you recommended, particularly [specific resource they mentioned].

Your generosity with your time and knowledge has made a significant impact on my pre-law journey. I'll be sure to keep you updated on my progress, and I hope our paths cross again in the future.

Warmly,

[Your Full Name]

[University] Class of [Year]

[Phone Number]

[Email Address]

Professional Communication Skills

IN THE LEGAL PROFESSION, how you communicate can be just as important as what you communicate. Mastering professional communication now will set you apart in your applications and prepare you for success in law school and beyond.

Crafting Emails That Get Responses

The ability to write clear, concise emails that prompt action is invaluable. Follow these principles:

Subject Line Strategy:

- Be specific and action-oriented: "Question about Summer Legal Internship Application" is better than "Question"
- Include deadlines if relevant: "Meeting Request: Available This Week"
- For cold emails, create interest: "Pre-Law Student Seeking Environmental Law Insight"

Email Structure:

- Brief, relevant greeting: "Dear Professor Smith," or "Hello Ms. Johnson,"
- Clear purpose statement: Start with one sentence explaining why you're writing
- Concise context: 2-3 sentences of relevant background
- Specific request: Exactly what you want (information, meeting, etc.)
- Proposed next steps or timeline: Make action easy
- Professional closing: "Thank you for your consideration," "Looking forward to your response"
- Complete signature: Your name, university, expected graduation, contact information

Tone and Style:

- Formal but not stiff: Avoid slang but don't use unnecessarily complex language

- Confident but respectful: "I would appreciate the opportunity to meet" rather than "I was hoping maybe we could meet if you're not too busy"
- Error-free: Proofread carefully for spelling, grammar, and formatting issues

Email Templates for Common Situations

Requesting an Informational Interview:

Subject: Environmental Law Career Insights - Meeting Request

Dear Ms. Johnson,

I am a junior at [University] pursuing a pre-law track with a focus on environmental studies. Your work with the Environmental Defense Fund, particularly the recent Mississippi River Basin project, aligns closely with my interest in water protection legislation.

Would you be willing to meet for 20 minutes, either virtually or at your office, to discuss your career path and any advice for someone interested in environmental law? I'm available Tuesdays and Thursdays after 2pm in the coming weeks.

Thank you for considering this request. I understand you're busy and appreciate any time you can offer.

Sincerely,

[Your Name]

[University] Class of [Year]

[Phone Number]

[Email Address]

Following Up After No Response:

Subject: Following Up: Environmental Law Career Insights

Dear Ms. Johnson,

I'm following up on my email from [date] regarding the possibility of a brief meeting to discuss your experience in environmental law. I understand you have a busy schedule, so I wanted to reiterate my interest and flexibility.

I would value even 15 minutes of your time, either in person or by phone. If meeting isn't possible, I would be grateful for any written advice you might share about entering the environmental law field.

Thank you for considering my request.

Best regards,
[Your Name]
[University] Class of [Year]
[Phone Number]
[Email Address]

Requesting a Recommendation Letter:

Subject: Recommendation Request for Law School Applications

Dear Professor Smith,

I hope this email finds you well. I'm preparing to apply to law schools this fall and would be honored if you would consider writing a letter of recommendation on my behalf.

As a student in your Constitutional Law seminar last spring, where I earned an A and wrote my term paper on First Amendment implications of social media regulation, I believe you could speak to my analytical abilities and writing skills. I've also served as your research assistant for the past semester, working on your judicial decision-making project.

If you're willing, I would provide you with my resume, personal statement draft, and a list of specific experiences or skills you might highlight. My applications are due December 1, so I would need the letter by November 15.

I understand writing recommendations requires significant time and effort. Please let me know if you would like to discuss this further or need additional information to consider my request.

Thank you for your consideration.

Respectfully,
[Your Name]
[University] Class of [Year]
[Phone Number]
[Email Address]

Subject: Request for Pre-Law Advising Appointment

Dear [Advisor Name],

I am a [year] [major] student at [University] interested in pursuing law school after graduation. I would like to schedule an appointment to discuss my pre-law path and get guidance on [specific topics, such as course selection, LSAT preparation, or application timeline].

I am available [provide specific days/times] in the coming weeks. If these times don't work with your schedule, please let me know what might be more convenient for you.

Before our meeting, I would appreciate knowing if there are any materials I should prepare or bring to make our discussion more productive.

Thank you for your time and assistance. I look forward to meeting with you.

Sincerely,

[Your Full Name]

[Student ID if relevant]

[University] Class of [Year]

[Phone Number]

[Email Address]

Subject: Question Regarding [Assignment/Concept] in [Course Name]

Dear Professor [Name],

I hope this email finds you well. I am a student in your [Course Name] class this semester and am seeking clarification on [specific assignment or concept].

After reviewing the [lecture notes/textbook/assignment guidelines], I understand that [what you do understand]. However, I'm unclear about [specific question or point of confusion].

I have attempted to resolve this by [what you've already tried - checking the syllabus, asking classmates, reviewing readings, etc.], but would appreciate your guidance on this matter.

Would it be possible to discuss this during your office hours on [day/time], or would you prefer to clarify via email?

Thank you for your time and assistance.

Respectfully,

[Your Full Name]

[Student ID if relevant]

[Course and Section Number]

[Email Address]

Personalize each template with specific details about your situation and the recipient.

Proofread carefully before sending—typos and grammatical errors undermine your professionalism.

Keep emails concise and focused on a single purpose or request.

Use a professional email address, ideally one with your name rather than a nickname or random numbers.

Include a clear subject line that previews the email's purpose.

Follow up respectfully if you don't receive a response within 1-2 weeks.

Express genuine appreciation for the recipient's time and assistance.

Save successful emails as templates for future use.

Remember that every email you send contributes to your professional reputation. These templates provide starting points, but your authentic voice and specific situation should shape your final communication.

Beyond Email: Other Professional Communication Contexts

Phone Calls:

- Prepare talking points before calling
- Identify yourself clearly: "Hello, this is [Name], a pre-law student at [University]"
- State your purpose concisely
- If leaving a voicemail, keep it under 30 seconds and include your phone number
- Follow up with an email summarizing any conversation

Video Meetings:

- Test technology beforehand
- Dress professionally from head to toe (you never know when you'll need to stand up)
- Choose a clean, well-lit background
- Look at the camera, not the screen, to maintain "eye contact"
- Minimize distractions and background noise

Thank You Notes:

- Send within 24-48 hours of a meeting or interview
- Reference specific points from your conversation
- Reiterate your interest and any next steps

- Consider handwritten notes for special circumstances (interviews, significant mentoring)

Consider Michael, who was nervous about reaching out to attorneys. He created templates for different situations, practiced with his pre-law advisor, and started with "warm" contacts (alumni from his university) before approaching strangers. Within three months, he had conducted ten informational interviews that helped him narrow his legal interests and build connections at his target law schools.

Professional communication isn't just about following formulas—it's about respecting others' time while clearly expressing your needs and interests. Master these skills now, and you'll stand out at every stage of your legal journey.

Here are some great books you can use to master your communication skills.

"Point Made: How to Write Like the Nation's Top Advocates" by Ross Guberman

Study the writing techniques of top lawyers through practical examples and explanations. This book will help you develop a clear, persuasive writing style that will serve you in personal statements, law school exams, and legal practice.

"Thank You for Arguing" by Jay Heinrichs

This entertaining guide to rhetoric and persuasion teaches practical techniques for constructing compelling arguments. Understanding these principles will improve your personal statement, strengthen your LSAT writing sample, and prepare you for the persuasive writing expected in law school.

"Bird by Bird" by Anne Lamott

Though not specifically about legal writing, this classic on the writing process offers invaluable wisdom for tackling large writing projects—like personal statements and law school exams—without becoming overwhelmed. Lamott's advice on "shitty first drafts" and taking things "bird by bird" will help you overcome perfectionism and writer's block.

"The Sense of Style" by Steven Pinker

This modern guide to clear, elegant writing will help you avoid the dense, convoluted style that plagues much legal writing. Pinker's cognitive approach to style will help you communicate complex ideas with clarity—a skill that distinguishes exceptional law students and attorneys.

"1L of a Ride" by Andrew J. McClurg

This candid guide to the first year of law school provides valuable insights into what to expect and how to succeed. Reading it before law school will help you hit the ground running with effective study strategies and realistic expectations.

"Whose Monet?: An Introduction to the American Legal System" by John Humbach

Through the story of a dispute over a painting, this book introduces the American legal system in an engaging, accessible way. It's an excellent primer on legal thinking and the court system for pre-law students.

"Just Mercy" by Bryan Stevenson

This powerful memoir by a public interest attorney illuminates both the challenges and the profound impact of legal advocacy. It offers an inspiring vision of how lawyers can work for justice while providing an unflinching look at the realities of our legal system.

"The Tools of Argument" by Joel P. Trachtman

Written by a law professor, this book breaks down the common forms of legal argument into accessible tools you can understand and apply. It's an excellent introduction to legal reasoning that will give you a head start on thinking like a lawyer.

Chapter 8: Design Your Health Strategy

Meal Prep Strategies

L aw school preparation demands intense mental energy, and your brain needs proper fuel to function at its best. Yet many pre-law students fall into the trap of sacrificing nutrition for study time, relying on vending machine snacks and delivery apps to get through LSAT prep and application season.

Strategic meal planning isn't just about health, it's about efficiency, budget management, and optimizing your brain performance. Here's how to fuel your pre-law journey without spending hours in the kitchen:

Brain-Boosting Nutrition Basics

Focus on incorporating these cognitive enhancers into your meals:

- Omega-3 fatty acids (salmon, walnuts, flaxseeds) support brain function
- Antioxidant-rich berries protect brain cells from stress damage
- Leafy greens provide folate for mental clarity
- Whole grains offer steady energy without crashes
- Lean proteins provide the building blocks for neurotransmitters
- Hydration is crucial—even mild dehydration impairs concentration

Weekly Meal Planning System

The key to consistent healthy eating is having a system:

Schedule 30 minutes each weekend for planning:

- Review your upcoming week's schedule
- Identify high-stress days that need grab-and-go options

- Plan 3-4 core meals to rotate throughout the week
- Create a master grocery list:
- Organize by store sections to shop efficiently
- Include quantities to avoid waste
- Keep a running list on your phone for items as you run out
- Batch cook foundation ingredients:
- Prepare proteins (grilled chicken, hard-boiled eggs, beans)
- Cook grains (brown rice, quinoa)
- Wash and chop vegetables
- Store in clear containers for easy mixing and matching

Assemble, don't cook:

- Focus on meals that combine pre-prepped ingredients
- Use formulas rather than recipes (grain + protein + vegetable + sauce)

Time-Saving Meal Prep Approaches
The Sunday Power Hour:

- Spend 60-90 minutes preparing:
- One sheet pan meal (roasted vegetables with protein)
- One pot of soup or stew
- One grain salad that improves with time
- Portioned snack containers

The 30-Minute Daily System:

- 10 minutes morning prep (overnight oats, packed lunch)
- 20 minutes evening cooking (simple dinner plus next-day components)

The Freezer Strategy:

- When cooking, always make double and freeze half
- Portion in individual containers for grab-and-go meals

- Label with contents and date
- Rotate through your freezer "inventory" regularly

Simple Brain-Boosting Recipes
Make-Ahead Breakfast Options:

- Overnight oats with berries and walnuts
- Egg muffins with vegetables (bake in muffin tins, refrigerate for 4 days)
- Greek yogurt parfaits with granola and fruit
- Freezer-friendly breakfast burritos

Study Session Lunches:

- Mason jar salads (dressing on bottom, greens on top)
- Protein boxes (hard-boiled eggs, cheese, nuts, fruit)
- Grain bowls with roasted vegetables and tahini sauce
- Wraps with hummus, vegetables, and leftover protein

Quick Dinner Formulas:

- Sheet pan meals: protein + vegetables + olive oil + herbs (roast at 400°F)
- Stir-fry template: protein + vegetables + sauce over rice
- Loaded sweet potatoes with various toppings
- "Breakfast for dinner" options like vegetable frittatas

Strategic Grocery Shopping
Pantry Staples:

- Canned beans and tuna for quick protein
- Whole grains (brown rice, quinoa, oats)
- Nuts and seeds for healthy fats
- Olive oil and vinegars for dressings
- Spices and herbs for flavor without added sodium

Freezer Essentials:

- Frozen berries for smoothies and oatmeal
- Frozen vegetables for quick stir-fries
- Frozen shrimp or chicken portions
- Whole grain bread for quick toast meals

Fresh Items to Prioritize:

- Leafy greens for salads and smoothies
- Eggs for versatile protein
- In-season fruits for snacking
- Pre-cut vegetables when time is limited

Consider Jessica, who found herself relying on expensive takeout during LSAT prep. She implemented a simple Sunday prep system: cooking a batch of chicken, roasting vegetables, and preparing overnight oats. This 90-minute routine saved her money, improved her energy levels, and eliminated the mental load of daily food decisions during her busiest study weeks.

Nutrition isn't separate from your pre-law strategy—it's a fundamental component. By fueling your brain properly, you'll enhance your learning capacity, improve focus, and build healthy habits that will serve you throughout your legal career.

Sustainable Exercise Routines

PHYSICAL ACTIVITY ISN'T a luxury for pre-law students, it's a necessity. Exercise improves cognitive function, reduces stress, enhances sleep quality, and builds the stamina you'll need for long study sessions and eventually, law school exams. The challenge is creating a sustainable routine that fits into your already packed schedule.

The key word here is "sustainable." The perfect workout routine is the one you'll actually do consistently. Let's build an approach that works with your pre-law life, not against it.

Exercise for Brain Performance

Research shows that physical activity directly benefits the cognitive functions you need for LSAT success and law school preparation:

- Aerobic exercise increases blood flow to the brain, improving processing speed
- Regular physical activity enhances memory formation and retention
- Exercise reduces stress hormones that impair logical reasoning
- Movement breaks can improve focus and prevent mental fatigue

Finding Your Minimum Effective Dose

When time is limited, focus on the minimum amount of exercise needed for cognitive benefits:

- As little as 20 minutes of moderate activity can improve brain function
- Three 30-minute sessions per week is sufficient for maintaining fitness
- Even 5-minute movement breaks every hour during study sessions help

Time-Efficient Workout Options

Study Break Exercises (5-10 minutes):

- Bodyweight circuit: 1 minute each of squats, push-ups, lunges, plank
- Desk stretching routine to combat sitting fatigue
- Quick walk around the building or up/down several flights of stairs
- Jump rope intervals (30 seconds on, 30 seconds rest)

Short Workout Sessions (20-30 minutes):

- High-intensity interval training (HIIT): alternate 30 seconds intense effort with 30 seconds rest
- Tabata protocol: 20 seconds work, 10 seconds rest, 8 rounds (4 minutes total) of 2-4 exercises
- Express yoga flows focusing on stress relief and mental clarity
- Strength training supersets (pairing exercises with no rest between)

Active Transportation:

- Walk or bike to campus instead of driving
- Park farther from buildings to add steps
- Take stairs instead of elevators
- Schedule walking meetings for study groups

Integrating Exercise with Study

- Audio Learning During Movement:
- Listen to LSAT concept reviews while walking
- Review recorded class notes during light cardio
- Use text-to-speech for articles while stretching

Study-Exercise Pairing:

- Alternate 25 minutes of focused study with 5 minutes of movement
- Use exercise as a reward after completing study milestones
- Schedule workouts immediately after difficult study sessions to process information

Movement-Friendly Study Methods:

- Practice LSAT logic games while standing at a counter
- Record yourself explaining concepts and listen while walking
- Use a standing or treadmill desk for reading sessions

Overcoming Common Barriers

- For the "Too Busy" Barrier:
- Schedule exercise as non-negotiable appointments
- Attach workouts to existing habits (e.g., morning coffee routine)
- Break exercise into multiple short sessions throughout the day
- Prioritize sleep and exercise equally with study time

For the "Low Energy" Barrier:

- Start with gentle movement like walking or stretching
- Schedule workouts for your natural energy peaks
- Use the "five-minute rule"—commit to just five minutes and then decide whether to continue
- Find an accountability partner for regular check-ins

For the "Lack of Facilities" Barrier:

- Create a minimal home workout space (all you need is floor space and perhaps a mat)
- Utilize campus recreation facilities between classes
- Explore free online workout videos requiring no equipment
- Use everyday objects (books, water bottles) as weights

Consider Marcus, who struggled to maintain his exercise routine during LSAT preparation. He created a "study-move-study" pattern, setting a timer for 50 minutes of focused work followed by 10 minutes of movement. He kept a yoga mat and resistance band next to his desk for quick workout breaks. This approach actually improved his practice test scores while preventing the physical pain and mental fatigue he had experienced with marathon study sessions.

The goal isn't becoming a fitness enthusiast—it's using strategic movement to enhance your cognitive performance and wellbeing. Start small, be consistent, and remember that the time you "spend" on exercise pays dividends in improved focus, better retention, and enhanced stress management.

Sleep as Revolutionary Act

IN A CULTURE THAT OFTEN glorifies overwork and sleep deprivation, prioritizing sleep as a pre-law student is nothing short of revolutionary. While all-nighters might seem like a badge of honor, the truth is that adequate sleep is one of your most powerful tools for academic success and mental wellbeing.

This is especially true for future lawyers of color, who often face additional stressors and pressures. Sleep isn't just about rest—it's about cognitive justice, giving your brain the resources it needs to perform at its highest level despite systemic challenges.

The Cognitive Case for Sleep

Sleep directly impacts the brain functions essential for law school success:

- Memory consolidation occurs primarily during deep sleep
- Critical thinking and logical reasoning decline with sleep deprivation
- Emotional regulation suffers without adequate rest
- Focus and attention span decrease dramatically
- Learning efficiency plummets, meaning study hours become less productive

Research shows that sleeping 6 hours or less for two weeks produces cognitive impairment equivalent to staying awake for 24 hours straight. No amount of caffeine can fully compensate for this deficit.

Sleep Quality vs. Quantity

While 7-9 hours is the recommended range for adults, quality matters as much as quantity:

- Uninterrupted sleep cycles are more restorative than fragmented sleep
- Deep sleep and REM sleep serve different cognitive functions
- Consistent sleep schedules support your body's natural rhythms
- The hour before midnight may provide more restorative sleep than later hours

Creating Your Sleep Sanctuary

Your sleep environment significantly impacts your rest quality:
Physical Space Optimization:

- Keep your bedroom cool (65-68°F is ideal for most people)
- Ensure complete darkness (use blackout curtains if needed)
- Minimize noise or use white noise to mask disturbances
- Invest in a comfortable mattress and pillows that support your sleep position

- Remove electronic devices or cover their lights

Digital Boundaries:

- Establish a "screens off" time at least 30 minutes before bed
- Use night mode or blue light filters on necessary devices
- Keep phones outside the bedroom or in a designated spot away from your bed
- Use "do not disturb" settings during sleep hours

Pre-Sleep Rituals for Law Students

Develop a consistent wind-down routine that signals to your brain that it's time to transition from study mode to rest:

Cognitive Decompression:

- Write tomorrow's to-do list to clear your mind
- Journal briefly about completed tasks and remaining concerns
- Practice a "brain dump" of lingering thoughts
- Review one positive accomplishment from the day

Physical Relaxation:

- Take a warm shower or bath
- Practice gentle stretching or yoga
- Try progressive muscle relaxation (tensing and releasing muscle groups)
- Use deep breathing exercises (4-7-8 breathing works well)

Sensory Calming:

- Dim lights progressively as bedtime approaches
- Use calming scents like lavender
- Listen to relaxing music or nature sounds
- Drink caffeine-free tea (chamomile, valerian, or passionflower)

Managing Law School Preparation Challenges

For Test Anxiety Nights:

- Prepare a specific sleep routine for nights before exams or important deadlines
- Practice visualization of successful performance rather than reviewing material
- Set multiple alarms to reduce fear of oversleeping
- Remind yourself that sleep will improve performance more than last-minute cramming

For Racing Thoughts:

- Keep a notepad by your bed to capture ideas without using phone lights
- Try guided meditation specifically designed for sleep (many free apps available)
- Use the "cognitive shuffle" technique—think of random words starting with the same letter
- Listen to sleep stories or gentle audiobooks on a timer

For Inconsistent Schedules:

- Identify your core sleep hours and protect them regardless of schedule changes
- Use consistent wake-up times even when bedtimes must vary
- Create abbreviated but consistent sleep rituals for busy nights
- Plan strategic 20-minute naps when full sleep cycles aren't possible

Consider Amara, who struggled with insomnia during her LSAT preparation. She created a 30-minute pre-sleep ritual: 10 minutes of writing down lingering concerns, 10 minutes of gentle stretching, and 10 minutes of reading fiction (not on a screen). She also established a firm "no LSAT after 9pm" rule. Within two weeks, her sleep quality improved dramatically, and her practice test scores increased by 5 points.

Prioritizing sleep isn't laziness or luxury, it's a strategic decision that optimizes your cognitive performance. In a pre-law culture that often normalizes exhaustion, choosing adequate rest is indeed revolutionary, and it may be the most important study strategy you adopt.

Chapter 9: Elevate Your Application Game

Personal Statement Strategies

Your personal statement is perhaps the only opportunity in your application where the admissions committee hears directly from you—in your own voice, telling your own story. It's not just another essay; it's a strategic presentation of who you are and why you belong in their law school.

Think of your personal statement as a closing argument in a case where you're the attorney, your transcripts are evidence, and your recommenders are the witnesses. You're making an argument for your admission, and every word should serve that purpose.

A Note on Diversity and Race in Admissions

In 2023, the Supreme Court's decision in *Students for Fair Admissions v. Harvard* and *UNC* significantly limited how colleges and universities can consider race in admissions. What this means for your personal essay is important: while schools can't use race as a direct factor in admissions, you *can* share how your race, ethnicity, or cultural background has shaped your experiences, challenges, or perspective.

Admissions committees are still allowed to consider those lived experiences—how they influenced your character, resilience, leadership, or motivation to pursue law. In other words, you can't simply write, "Admit me because of my race," but you *can* show how your identity and the realities tied to it prepared you to contribute uniquely to the law school community.

A Note on Using AI for Writing During this Process

Artificial intelligence has quickly become a go-to tool for students at every level, and law school applicants are no exception. From brainstorming ideas for personal essays to polishing up recommendation letters or scholarship applications, AI can feel like the best study buddy you never had. It can help you outline your thoughts, structure your arguments, and catch those pesky grammar mistakes that spellcheck misses. For students juggling LSAT prep, work, and life, having a tool that speeds up the writing process can feel like a lifesaver.

But here's the catch: AI is only as good as the instructions you give it—and even then, it can go left real quick. These tools are known to "hallucinate," meaning they make up information that looks official but isn't true. That's a problem if you're letting AI write your personal essay or, worse, fabricate details in a recommendation letter. Law school admissions officers are lawyers and professors by training. Translation: they can smell inconsistencies a mile away. What seems like a polished essay could actually raise red flags if the details don't add up or the voice doesn't sound like you.

Another major pitfall? The admissions committee isn't just reading your personal essay in isolation. They're comparing it to your LSAT writing sample and every other piece of writing in your application. If your personal statement reads like it came from a seasoned novelist but your LSAT writing sample looks like it came from someone still warming up their legal writing muscles, the contrast will be obvious. Authenticity matters. Committees aren't expecting perfection, they're expecting you.

So, use AI wisely. Think of it as a proofreader, a brainstorming partner, or even a way to organize your ideas more clearly. But don't let it do the heavy lifting. Your personal statement is one of the only places in the application where you can show who you really are, beyond scores and transcripts. Let AI tidy up the edges, but make sure your story, your voice, and your truth are at the center. That's the kind of essay that stands out, and the kind of applicant law schools want to admit.

Strong recommendation letters can elevate your application from good to outstanding. By strategically selecting recommenders and supporting them with the right materials, you ensure these external voices effectively advocate for your admission.

Finding Your Authentic Story

The most compelling personal statements emerge from genuine self-reflection. Before writing, explore these questions:

- What experiences have shaped your interest in law? (Look beyond the obvious "I've always wanted to be a lawyer" narrative).
- What challenges have you overcome that demonstrate qualities valuable in legal education?
- What perspective or background would you bring to a law school classroom?
- How have you demonstrated commitment to your goals?
- What values drive your interest in the legal profession?

The best topics often emerge from the intersection of what makes you unique and what makes you well-suited for legal education.

Strategic Sharing vs. Trauma Dumping

Many applicants feel pressure to share painful personal experiences to stand out. While adversity can shape powerful narratives, consider these guidelines:

Strategic sharing:

- Focuses on your response to challenges rather than the challenges themselves.
- Demonstrates growth, resilience, and lessons learned.
- Connects past experiences to future legal aspirations.
- Includes reflection on how these experiences will inform your approach to law.

Avoid trauma dumping:

- Sharing traumatic experiences without context or reflection.
- Using hardship as the sole justification for admission.
- Including graphic or disturbing details unnecessarily.
- Writing about unprocessed trauma that you're still working through.

Remember: The admissions committee isn't looking for the applicant who has suffered most, but for candidates who demonstrate the qualities needed for law school success.

Structural Approaches That Work

While there's no single "correct" format, these structures often create compelling narratives:

The Defining Moment:

- Open with a specific scene that catalyzed your interest in law.
- Expand to show how this moment connects to your broader journey.
- Conclude by linking this experience to your legal aspirations.

The Evolution:

- Trace the development of your interest in law over time.
- Highlight key turning points or realizations.
- Show how your understanding has matured and deepened.

The Thematic Approach:

- Identify a core quality relevant to legal education (analytical thinking, advocacy, etc.).
- Illustrate this quality through 2-3 different experiences.
- Connect this theme to your potential contribution to the law school.

The Why Law/Why Now:

- Particularly effective for career-changers or non-traditional applicants.
- Explain how your previous experiences led logically to law.
- Address the timing of your decision to pursue legal education.

Writing Techniques That Elevate Your Statement
Show, don't just tell:

- Use specific scenes and sensory details.
- Include dialogue where appropriate.
- Provide concrete examples rather than general claims.

Create a narrative arc:

- Ensure your statement has a beginning, middle, and end.
- Build toward insights or realizations.
- Leave the reader with a clear sense of your trajectory.

Find your authentic voice:

- Write how you speak (but more polished).
- Avoid legal jargon or overly formal language.
- Read your draft aloud to check for authenticity.

Edit ruthlessly:

- Every paragraph should advance your argument for admission.
- Cut any sentence that doesn't add new information.
- Eliminate clichés and generic statements about "passion for justice."

Writing Prompts to Get Started
If you're facing a blank page, try these prompts to generate material:

- Describe a moment when you realized the power of law or advocacy.
- Write about a time when you changed your mind about something important.
- Reflect on an experience that tested your values or beliefs.
- Describe a problem you've worked to solve and what you learned from the process.
- Write about a person who influenced your understanding of justice or fairness.

Consider Maria, who struggled with her personal statement until she focused on her experience mediating conflicts in her large, multigenerational household? Rather than writing generally about "communication skills," she described specific scenes that demonstrated her ability to understand different perspectives and find common ground—qualities essential for legal practice.

Your personal statement should leave the admissions committee thinking, "This is someone who will add value to our community and succeed in our program." With thoughtful reflection and strategic presentation, your authentic story becomes compelling evidence for your admission.

Resume Building Techniques

YOUR LAW SCHOOL RESUME isn't just a history of your jobs and activities—it's a strategic document that highlights the skills and experiences most relevant to legal education. Unlike a standard professional resume, a law school resume should emphasize academic achievements, analytical abilities, and leadership experiences.

Strategic Content Selection

Law schools look for specific qualities in applicants. Highlight experiences that demonstrate:

- Research and analytical skills
- Writing and communication abilities
- Leadership and initiative
- Time management and organization
- Commitment to service or justice
- Perseverance through challenges

For each entry on your resume, ask: *"What does this experience show about my potential as a law student?"* If you can't clearly answer that question, consider whether the entry deserves space on your resume.

Formatting for Maximum Impact

Overall Structure:

Length: 1-2 pages (2 pages is acceptable for applicants with significant work experience)

Margins: 0.75-1 inch all around

Font: Professional and readable (Times New Roman, Calibri, or similar)

Font size: 10-12 point for body text, slightly larger for headings

Consistency: Use the same formatting for similar elements throughout

Section Order:

For most pre-law students, this order works well:

- Contact information and education
- Honors and awards
- Relevant experience (legal, research, writing, advocacy)
- Additional work experience
- Leadership and activities
- Skills and interests (if space allows)

For applicants with significant work experience, professional experience may come before education.

Education Section Strategies

Include:

- Full name of institution and location
- Degree earned or pursuing with expected graduation date
- Major(s), minor(s), and concentration(s)
- GPA (overall and major if significantly higher)
- Academic honors (Dean's List, Latin honors)
- Relevant coursework (3-5 courses most relevant to law)
- Study abroad experiences
- Thesis or capstone project titles

Example:

EDUCATION

University of Michigan, Ann Arbor, MI

Bachelor of Arts in Political Science, Minor in Economics, May 2023

GPA: 3.82/4.00 (Dean's List: 6 semesters)

Relevant Coursework: Constitutional Law, Logic and Critical Thinking, Research Methods

Honors Thesis: "First Amendment Implications of Social Media Content Moderation"

Experience Section Techniques

For each position, include:

- Organization name and location
- Your title or role

- Dates of involvement (month/year to month/year)
- 2-4 bullet points describing accomplishments, not just responsibilities

Use the CAR method for bullet points:

- Challenge: What problem or situation did you face?
- Action: What specific actions did you take?
- Result: What was the outcome or impact?

Use strong action verbs:

- Research skills: analyzed, investigated, evaluated, examined
- Writing skills: authored, composed, drafted, edited
- Leadership: directed, coordinated, managed, supervised
- Problem-solving: resolved, implemented, developed, created

Example:
LEGAL EXPERIENCE
District Attorney's Office, Philadelphia, PA
Undergraduate Intern, May 2022 - August 2022
- Researched case law for 15+ misdemeanor cases, creating summary briefs for assistant district attorneys
- Organized witness statements and evidence for 3 felony trials, ensuring all materials were properly cataloged
- Observed court proceedings daily, including arraignments, preliminary hearings, and trials

Highlighting Pre-Law Relevant Activities
Even experiences not explicitly "legal" can demonstrate relevant skills:
Academic Research:

- Detail your role in the research process
- Emphasize analytical methods used
- Mention any resulting publications or presentations

Student Government:

- Focus on policy development or conflict resolution
- Quantify your impact when possible
- Highlight collaboration with diverse stakeholders

Volunteer Work:

- Emphasize advocacy or educational components
- Detail any training or specialized knowledge acquired
- Show commitment through consistent involvement

Skills and Additional Information

Languages:

Specify proficiency level (native, fluent, proficient, conversational)

Include relevant certifications or formal study

Technical Skills:

- Research databases you've used (JSTOR, LexisNexis)
- Data analysis tools or programming languages
- Advanced software proficiency beyond basics

Interests (optional):

Include only if they add dimension to your application

Focus on interests that show depth or commitment

Avoid generic listings like "reading" or "travel"

Consider Jordan, whose initial resume listed his restaurant server job with generic duties like "took orders" and "served food." He revised it to highlight transferable skills: "Managed multiple time-sensitive tasks simultaneously in a high-pressure environment" and "Resolved customer concerns diplomatically, maintaining a 95% satisfaction rating." This reframing showed his ability to perform under pressure and handle interpersonal conflicts—valuable skills for future lawyers.

Your resume should tell a coherent story about who you are and why you're prepared for the rigors of legal education. Every element should contribute to that narrative, presenting you as a candidate who will thrive in law school and beyond.

Recommendation Letter Guide

STRONG RECOMMENDATION letters provide external validation of your abilities and potential, they're like character witnesses in the case for your admission. But securing effective letters requires strategy and thoughtfulness, not just asking the first professors who come to mind.

Choosing the Right Recommenders

- The best letters come from people who:
- Know you well enough to provide specific examples
- Have observed you in academically rigorous situations
- Can speak to qualities relevant to law school success
- Hold positions that lend credibility to their assessment

Typically, you'll need 2-3 letters, with at least two from academic sources. Consider these potential recommenders:

- Academic Sources (Primary):
- Professors from smaller, discussion-based classes
- Research mentors or thesis advisors
- Professors from writing-intensive courses
- Academic advisors who know you beyond basic advising
- Professional Sources (Supplementary):
- Supervisors from legal internships
- Employers who have observed your analytical skills
- Research directors or lab managers
- Volunteer coordinators for substantial commitments

Avoid these common recommendation mistakes:

- Choosing famous professors who barely know you
- Selecting easy A professors who can't speak to your ability to handle challenges
- Using family friends with impressive titles but little relevant knowledge of your abilities

- Relying on character references who can only speak to your personal qualities

Approaching Potential Recommenders

How you ask can significantly impact the quality of your letters:

Timing:

- Make initial requests at least 2-3 months before deadlines
- Approach professors during the semester, not during breaks
- Consider asking at the end of a course while your work is still fresh in their minds

Method:

- Request in person when possible (office hours are ideal)
- If in-person isn't possible, email to schedule a virtual meeting
- Avoid asking via quick emails or after class

The Ask:

Be direct but respectful: "Would you feel comfortable writing a strong letter of recommendation for my law school applications?"

The phrasing matters—it gives them an out if they don't feel they can write a compelling letter

Be prepared for questions about your law school plans

If they say yes:

- Express genuine appreciation.
- Discuss next steps and timeline.
- Schedule a follow-up meeting or email to provide materials.
- Ask the if they are comfortable with you creating the first draft of the recommendation letter.

If they decline:

- Thank them for their honesty.
- Understand that a lukewarm letter would hurt your application.

- Ask if they can suggest someone else who might know your work better.

Providing Materials to Recommenders

Help your recommenders write detailed, specific letters by providing:
Essential Documents:

- Your current resume
- Personal statement draft (even if still in progress)
- Transcript (unofficial is fine)
- List of schools and deadlines
- Submission instructions
- Personalized Reminder Sheet:
- Courses taken with them, including semester and year
- Grades received and major assignments/papers
- Research or projects completed under their supervision
- Class discussions or office hour conversations that were meaningful
- How their course or mentorship influenced your interest in law

Suggestion Sheet (optional but helpful):

Specific qualities you hope they might address (analytical skills, writing ability, etc.)

- Particular experiences or assignments that demonstrated these qualities
- Connections between their observations and your law school goals

Managing the Process

- Timeline Management:
- Create a spreadsheet tracking each recommender, school, and deadline
- Send gentle reminders 3-4 weeks and 1-2 weeks before deadlines
- Offer to meet again if they need additional information

Using LSAC's CAS System:

- Register recommenders in the system early
- Provide clear instructions for uploading letters
- Explain whether you're using general or school-specific letters

Following Up:

- Send thank-you notes after letters are submitted
- Keep recommenders updated on your application results
- Share your final decision and express appreciation again

Handling Awkward Situations

For recommenders who are slow to respond:

- Send polite reminder emails with specific deadlines
- Offer to meet to provide additional information
- Have a backup recommender in mind if necessary

For recommenders who ask you to draft your own letter:

- Recognize this is not uncommon but requires careful handling
- Write a factual, specific letter highlighting your actual accomplishments
- Avoid excessive self-praise or language you wouldn't use
- Provide it as a "starting point" they can modify

Consider Tanya, who was nervous about asking her constitutional law professor for a recommendation. She scheduled an office hours appointment, brought her graded papers from the course, and explained specifically why his assessment would be valuable (he had seen her analytical writing and class participation). She then provided a detailed reminder sheet about her work in his class. The resulting letter specifically addressed her ability to construct logical arguments and respond to criticism—exactly the qualities law schools value.

Sample Email Requesting Recommendation Letter

Subject: Recommendation Request for Law School Applications

Dear Professor [Name],

I hope this email finds you well. I am preparing to apply to law schools this fall and would be honored if you would consider writing a letter of recommendation on my behalf.

As a student in your [course name] course during [semester/year], where I earned [grade], I believe you could speak to my [specific skills relevant to law school, such as analytical abilities, writing skills, or class participation]. [Add a specific memory or project from the class that the professor might remember].

If you feel comfortable providing a recommendation, I would be happy to share my resume, personal statement draft, and a list of my relevant experiences and accomplishments to make the process easier for you. My applications are due [deadline date], so I would need the letter by [date at least 2-3 weeks before deadline].

I understand writing recommendations requires significant time and effort. Please let me know if you would like to discuss this further or need additional information to consider my request.

Thank you for your consideration.

Respectfully,

[Your Full Name]

[Student ID if relevant]

[University] Class of [Year]

[Phone Number]

[Email Address]

Chapter 10: Parents and Caretakers

Parents

Navigating the pre-law journey isn't a solo act; for many, parents and caretakers are integral members of the support crew, sometimes even feeling like the stage managers of the whole production. This chapter is dedicated to understanding and optimizing that relationship, acknowledging that parental involvement can be both a blessing and, at times, a source of added pressure. Whether your parents are your biggest cheerleaders, concerned sideline coaches, or something in between, understanding their perspective and setting healthy boundaries is essential for your well-being and your success.

Let's start by acknowledging the elephant in the room: expectations. Parents often have dreams and aspirations for their children, shaped by their own experiences, values, and hopes for a secure future. For some, law school represents the pinnacle of achievement, a path to stability, prestige, and influence. They might see your acceptance into a good law school as a validation of their parenting efforts, a return on their investment in your education, or even a way to fulfill their own unfulfilled ambitions. It's essential to remember that their expectations, even if they feel burdensome, usually stem from a place of love and a genuine desire for your happiness.

However, those expectations can manifest in ways that are less than helpful. Constant questioning about your LSAT score, unsolicited advice about your personal statement, or pressure to apply to specific schools can all contribute to your stress levels and erode your confidence. The key here is open and honest communication. Sit down with your parents and have a conversation about your goals, your anxieties, and the kind of support you need from them.

Explain that while you appreciate their interest and concern, their constant monitoring or unsolicited advice is actually hindering your progress.

Frame the conversation in a way that emphasizes your shared goals. For example, instead of saying, "Stop asking me about the LSAT," try something like, "I know you want me to do well on the LSAT, and I appreciate that. But honestly, every time you ask, it just makes me more anxious, which actually makes it harder for me to study. What would really help me is if you could trust that I'm doing my best and offer encouragement instead."

Setting boundaries is another vital aspect of managing parental involvement. This might mean establishing specific times when you're available to talk about law school, or creating a "no law school talk" zone during family gatherings. It's about carving out space for yourself where you can focus on your studies and your well-being without feeling constantly scrutinized or pressured.

It's also important to manage the flow of information. You don't need to share every detail of your pre-law journey with your parents. Choose what you share based on what you feel comfortable discussing and what you believe will be helpful to them. For example, you might share your study schedule or your list of target schools, but keep the details of your practice test scores or your drafts of your personal statement to yourself until you feel ready to get their feedback.

Now, let's flip the script and consider the positive aspects of parental involvement. Parents can be incredible sources of support, both emotionally and practically. They can offer a listening ear, provide words of encouragement, help with logistical tasks, or even offer financial assistance. The key is to identify the ways in which they can best support you and to communicate your needs clearly.

Perhaps you could ask your parents to help you with meal prepping, so you have more time to study. Or maybe you could ask them to proofread your personal statement, offering a fresh perspective on your writing. If you're feeling overwhelmed, you could simply ask them to listen to your concerns and offer a shoulder to cry on.

Remember, your parents have likely accumulated a wealth of life experience, and they may have valuable insights to offer, even if they don't have direct experience with the legal field. They can help you think through problems, manage your time effectively, and stay focused on your goals.

Furthermore, involving your parents in your pre-law journey can strengthen your relationship with them. By sharing your aspirations and challenges, you're inviting them into your world and demonstrating that you value their opinions and support. This can lead to deeper understanding, greater empathy, and a stronger bond between you and your parents.

However, it's important to acknowledge that not everyone has supportive or involved parents. Some students may face parents who are actively discouraging, uninvolved, or even abusive. In these situations, it's crucial to prioritize your own well-being and seek support from other sources.

If you're dealing with unsupportive parents, it's important to set firm boundaries and limit your contact with them as much as possible. Focus on building a support network of friends, mentors, and other trusted individuals who can provide you with the encouragement and guidance you need. Remember, you are not alone, and there are resources available to help you navigate these difficult situations.

For those students whose parents are not in the picture, whether through death, estrangement, or other circumstances, the pre-law journey can feel particularly isolating. It's important to acknowledge this feeling and to actively seek out surrogate parental figures or mentors who can provide guidance and support. This might be a favorite teacher, a family friend, or a professional in the legal field who is willing to take you under their wing.

Moreover, it's essential to recognize that the definition of "family" is fluid and can encompass a wide range of relationships. Your chosen family – the friends, partners, and mentors who support and uplift you – can be just as valuable as your biological family. Lean on these individuals for emotional support, practical assistance, and a sense of belonging.

In some cultures, family obligations and responsibilities take precedence over individual aspirations. Students from these backgrounds may feel torn between pursuing their own dreams and fulfilling their family's expectations. This can create a significant amount of stress and guilt, making the pre-law journey even more challenging.

If you're facing this dilemma, it's important to find a balance between honoring your family's values and pursuing your own goals. This might involve having open and honest conversations with your family about your aspirations, explaining why law school is important to you, and finding ways to compromise and meet their expectations while still pursuing your dreams.

Remember, it's possible to honor your cultural heritage and family obligations while still carving out your own path. It's about finding a way to integrate your family's values into your own life in a way that feels authentic and empowering.

Ultimately, the relationship with your parents and caretakers is a complex and dynamic one that requires ongoing communication, understanding, and boundary setting. By recognizing their perspective, communicating your needs, and seeking their support in a way that works for you, you can transform this relationship from a source of stress into a source of strength. The goal is to create a supportive and collaborative partnership that empowers you to thrive on your pre-law journey and beyond. Whether your parents are seasoned legal professionals or completely unfamiliar with the legal field, their love, support, and belief in you can be invaluable assets as you navigate the challenging but rewarding path to law school.

Parents of Young Children - Be Prepared

NAVIGATING THE PRE-law process with young children in tow is a Herculean task, a juggling act of epic proportions where law school aspirations often compete with diaper changes, bedtime stories, and the ever-present demands of tiny humans.

This isn't just about time management; it's about emotional bandwidth, mental resilience, and a radical redefinition of productivity. Forget the pristine study schedules and uninterrupted library sessions you envisioned. This is about embracing the chaos, finding slivers of time, and mastering the art of focused bursts of activity.

First, let's address the most obvious challenge: time. As a parent of young children, your time isn't just limited; it's fragmented. Days are punctuated by meals, naps, playdates, and the inevitable emergencies that come with raising kids. Finding dedicated study time requires creativity, strategic planning, and a willingness to sacrifice.

One key strategy is to identify your peak performance times. Are you a morning person? Try waking up an hour before the kids to squeeze in some focused study. Are you a night owl? Carve out time after they're in bed, even if it's just for an hour or two. Don't try to force yourself to study when you're exhausted or distracted; it's far more efficient to work in short bursts when you're fresh and alert.

Embrace the power of small pockets of time. Can you review flashcards during your child's soccer practice? Listen to LSAT podcasts while you're cooking dinner? Utilize nap times strategically, even if it means foregoing your own afternoon rest. Every little bit counts, and those small increments can add up over time.

Technology can be your ally. Utilize apps and online resources that allow you to study on the go. Download lectures to listen to during your commute, or use flashcard apps on your phone while you're waiting in line at the grocery store. The key is to integrate study into your daily routine, making it a seamless part of your life rather than a separate, overwhelming task.

Another strategy is to enlist support from your partner, family, or friends. If possible, negotiate dedicated study time with your partner, where they take on the primary childcare responsibilities. Ask grandparents or other relatives to babysit for a few hours each week. Consider hiring a part-time nanny or joining a babysitting co-op with other parents. Remember, it's okay to ask for help; you don't have to do everything alone.

Now, let's move on to the less obvious, but equally important, challenge: mental and emotional well-being. Parenting is demanding, and combining it with the rigors of pre-law preparation can take a significant toll on your mental health. It's easy to feel overwhelmed, stressed, and guilty – guilty about not spending enough time with your kids, guilty about not studying enough, guilty about not being "perfect" in either role.

The first step in managing your mental health is to acknowledge your limitations. You can't do everything, and you can't be everything to everyone. Accept that there will be days when you feel like you're failing, and that's okay. Give yourself permission to take breaks, to ask for help, and to prioritize your own well-being.

Practice self-compassion. Treat yourself with the same kindness and understanding that you would offer to a friend in the same situation. Remind yourself that you're doing your best, and that's enough. Avoid negative self-talk and perfectionistic tendencies. Focus on progress, not perfection.

Prioritize self-care. This isn't selfish; it's essential. Make time for activities that help you relax, recharge, and reconnect with yourself. This might be as simple as taking a hot bath, reading a book, going for a walk, or spending time with friends. Whatever it is, make sure it's something that nourishes your soul and helps you de-stress.

Mindfulness and meditation can be invaluable tools for managing stress and anxiety. Even a few minutes of daily mindfulness practice can help you center yourself, calm your mind, and improve your focus. There are numerous apps and online resources that offer guided meditations specifically designed for busy parents.

Exercise is another powerful stress reliever. Physical activity releases endorphins, which have mood-boosting effects. Even short bursts of exercise, like a brisk walk or a quick workout video, can make a difference. Incorporate movement into your daily routine whenever possible, whether it's playing with your kids in the park or taking the stairs instead of the elevator.

Nutrition plays a crucial role in mental well-being. Fuel your body with healthy, whole foods that provide sustained energy. Avoid processed foods, sugary drinks, and excessive caffeine, which can exacerbate stress and anxiety. Meal prepping can be a lifesaver for busy parents, allowing you to prepare healthy meals in advance and avoid the temptation of unhealthy takeout options.

Sleep is non-negotiable. While it may be tempting to sacrifice sleep in order to study, lack of sleep can actually impair cognitive function and worsen stress levels. Aim for at least seven to eight hours of sleep per night. Establish a consistent sleep schedule and create a relaxing bedtime routine to improve the quality of your sleep.

Another important aspect of navigating the pre-law journey as a parent is managing your children's expectations. They may not fully understand what you're doing, but they will sense your stress and absence. It's important to communicate with them in age-appropriate ways about your goals and your need for study time.

Explain to them that you're working hard to achieve something important, and that while it may mean spending less time with them in the short term, it will ultimately benefit your family in the long run. Involve them in your study process whenever possible. Let them see you reading and learning, and explain to them what you're studying. This can help them understand the value of education and instill a love of learning in them.

Make dedicated time for your children, even if it's just for a few minutes each day. Put away your phone and give them your undivided attention. Read them a story, play a game, or simply cuddle with them on the couch. These small moments of connection can make a big difference in their sense of security and your overall well-being.

Involve your children in household chores and responsibilities. This can help them learn valuable life skills and free up some of your time for studying. Delegate tasks that are appropriate for their age and abilities, such as setting the table, folding laundry, or helping with meal preparation.

Be present, even when you're not physically present. Technology allows you to stay connected with your children even when you're away from home. Send them a text message, call them during your lunch break, or schedule a video chat in the evening. These small gestures can help them feel loved and connected, even when you're busy.

Finally, remember that you are a role model for your children. By pursuing your dreams and working hard to achieve your goals, you're teaching them valuable lessons about perseverance, determination, and the importance of education. You're showing them that anything is possible if you set your mind to it, and that even parents can have dreams and aspirations. Your children will be proud of you, and they will learn from your example.

Caretakers- Everyone Needs to be on board

IT'S LIKE TRYING TO solve a Rubik's Cube while riding a unicycle on a tightrope when you're venturing into the pre-law process as a caretaker – you're not just managing your own ambitions, but also the well-being of others who depend on you. This journey is a team effort, and getting everyone on board isn't just helpful, it's essential for your success and sanity.

Let's be real, being a caretaker already puts you in BEST MODE due to endurance, swagger, and tenacity. You're used to juggling multiple roles, anticipating needs, and making tough decisions. Now, it's time to apply those skills to your pre-law journey, making sure your loved ones understand and support your aspirations.

One of the first and most important steps is open and honest communication. Don't assume your family knows what law school entails or why you want to pursue this path. Sit down with them and explain your goals, aspirations, and the impact this decision will have on your life and theirs.

Start by sharing your "why." Why do you want to go to law school? What motivates you? What impact do you hope to make in the world? Sharing your personal connection to the legal profession will help your family understand your commitment and passion.

Next, address the practical aspects of your decision. Explain the time commitment involved in studying for the LSAT, preparing applications, and eventually attending law school. Be transparent about the financial implications, including tuition costs, living expenses, and potential lost income.

It's also important to acknowledge the impact on your family's daily life. Will you need more help with household chores or childcare? Will you be less available for social activities? Will you need a quiet space to study? Addressing these issues upfront will help avoid misunderstandings and resentment down the road.

When communicating with your family, be prepared to answer questions and address concerns. They may worry about the financial burden, the time commitment, or the stress you'll be under. Listen to their concerns with empathy and validate their feelings.

Provide reassurance and offer solutions. For example, if they're worried about the financial impact, discuss your plans for financial aid, scholarships, and budgeting. If they're concerned about the time commitment, explore ways to share responsibilities and create a supportive environment.

Remember, communication is a two-way street. Ask your family what they need from you during this time. How can you support them while pursuing your goals? What are their expectations? Finding a balance that works for everyone is key.

Setting expectations is another crucial aspect of getting your family on board. Be clear about what you can and cannot do. Don't overpromise or try to be a superhero. It's okay to say no to commitments that will stretch you too thin.

Establish boundaries and prioritize your time. Designate specific study times and let your family know that you need uninterrupted time during those periods. Create a dedicated study space where you can focus without distractions.

Delegate tasks whenever possible. Enlist your partner, children, or other family members to help with household chores, errands, and childcare. Don't be afraid to ask for help; it's a sign of strength, not weakness.

It's also important to manage expectations about your performance. Law school is challenging, and there will be times when you struggle or feel overwhelmed. Don't put undue pressure on yourself to be perfect. Focus on progress, not perfection, and celebrate your accomplishments along the way.

One powerful strategy is to involve your family in your pre-law journey. This can help them feel more connected to your goals and more invested in your success.

Share your study materials with them. Explain the concepts you're learning and ask them to quiz you. This can be a fun and engaging way to involve them in your studies and help them understand what you're going through.

Attend pre-law events and information sessions together. This will give your family a better understanding of the law school application process and the legal profession. It will also allow them to meet other pre-law students and their families, creating a sense of community and support.

If possible, take your family on a visit to a law school campus. This will give them a firsthand look at the environment you'll be studying in and help them visualize your future.

Another effective way to get your family on board is to highlight the benefits of your pursuing law school. Emphasize the positive impact it will have on your family's future.

Explain how a law degree will open doors to new career opportunities and increased financial stability. Share your vision for how you'll use your legal skills to make a difference in the world and contribute to your community.

Show your family how your pursuing law school will benefit them personally. Will it allow you to provide a better education for your children?

Will it enable you to support your aging parents? Will it give you more time and resources to spend with your loved ones?

When you can demonstrate the tangible benefits of your decision, your family will be more likely to support your goals.

Seeking support from other caretakers who have gone through the pre-law process can be invaluable. Connect with other parents, spouses, or caregivers who are pursuing or have pursued legal careers.

Join online communities and forums where you can share your experiences, ask questions, and offer advice. Attend networking events and meetups for pre-law students and legal professionals with families.

These connections can provide a sense of camaraderie and understanding, as well as practical tips and strategies for balancing your responsibilities.

Don't underestimate the power of professional support. Consider hiring a tutor or academic coach to help you with the LSAT and application process. Work with a therapist or counselor to manage stress and maintain your mental health.

Investing in professional support can alleviate some of the burden on your family and ensure that you have the resources you need to succeed.

It's also okay to adjust your timeline. The pre-law journey doesn't have to be a sprint; it can be a marathon. If you need to take a break to focus on your family or other commitments, that's perfectly acceptable.

Be flexible and adaptable. Life happens, and you may need to adjust your plans along the way. Don't be afraid to modify your timeline, re-prioritize your goals, or seek out alternative paths to law school.

The most important thing is to stay true to your vision and keep moving forward, even if it's at a slower pace.

Most importantly, remember to take care of yourself. You can't pour from an empty cup. Prioritize your physical, mental, and emotional well-being.

Schedule regular exercise, eat healthy meals, and get enough sleep. Make time for activities that you enjoy and that help you relax and recharge.

Practice mindfulness and self-compassion. Be kind to yourself and acknowledge your accomplishments. Remember that you're doing your best, and that's enough.

When you prioritize your own well-being, you'll be better equipped to handle the challenges of the pre-law journey and to support your family along the way.

Navigating the pre-law process as a caretaker is undoubtedly challenging, but it's also incredibly rewarding. By communicating openly, setting expectations, involving your family, seeking support, and taking care of yourself, you can create a supportive environment that enables you to pursue your dreams and achieve your goals. Remember, you're not just pursuing a legal career; you're building a better future for yourself and your loved ones. That's a BE§T MODE win for everyone.

Spouses and Significant Others - Get Buy In Early

NAVIGATING THE PRE-law path is like embarking on an epic quest, but it's a quest that often impacts not just you, but also the people closest to you – especially your spouse or significant other. Their support, or lack thereof, can truly make or break your journey, so let's talk about how to get them on board early.

Think of it as building a sturdy foundation before constructing a skyscraper. You wouldn't just start stacking steel beams without ensuring the ground beneath is solid, right? Similarly, you can't expect to dive headfirst into LSAT prep and law school applications without having a heart-to-heart with your partner about the journey ahead.

First, understand that their initial reaction might not be all sunshine and rainbows. It's easy to get caught up in your own excitement and forget that your decision impacts them, too. They might have concerns about the financial strain, the time commitment, or the changes in your daily routines. So, prepare yourself to listen, truly listen, to their worries and validate their feelings. Don't dismiss their concerns as silly or unimportant, even if you don't agree with them. Acknowledge that their life is changing, too.

Now, let's break down how to communicate effectively. It's not just about what you say, but how you say it. Approach the conversation with empathy and understanding. Put yourself in their shoes and try to see things from their perspective.

Start by sharing your "why." This is crucial. Don't just say, "I want to go to law school." Tell them why. What drives you? What are your aspirations? What kind of impact do you hope to make? Share your vision for the future and how a legal career fits into that vision. When they understand your passion and your purpose, they're more likely to support your goals.

Next, be transparent about the realities of the pre-law process. Explain the time commitment involved in studying for the LSAT, preparing applications, and eventually attending law school. Be honest about the financial implications, including tuition costs, living expenses, and potential lost income. Don't sugarcoat anything, but also don't dwell on the negatives. Present a realistic picture of what lies ahead, both the challenges and the rewards.

Talk about how your pursuit of law school will affect your daily life together. Will you need more help with household chores or childcare? Will you be less available for social activities? Will you need a quiet space to study? Addressing these issues upfront will help avoid misunderstandings and resentment down the road. The goal here is to paint a picture of what the new normal might look like, so you both can prepare and adjust.

When you talk with your partner, be ready to answer questions and address their worries. They might worry about the financial burden, the time commitment, or the stress you'll be under. Listen to their concerns with empathy and validate their feelings. Let them know that you understand their concerns and that you're committed to finding solutions together.

Offer reassurance and suggest ways to ease their worries. For instance, if they're worried about the financial impact, talk about your plans for financial aid, scholarships, and budgeting. If they're concerned about the time commitment, explore ways to share responsibilities and create a supportive environment. Make them a part of the solution, and it will become a shared journey.

Keep in mind that communication is a two-way street. Ask your partner what they need from you during this time. How can you support them while pursuing your goals? What are their expectations? Finding a balance that works for both of you is key. This isn't a dictatorship; it's a partnership.

It's time to set some expectations. Be clear about what you can and cannot do. Don't overpromise or try to be a superhero. It's okay to say no to commitments that will stretch you too thin. Establishing boundaries and prioritizing your time is crucial for maintaining your sanity and your relationship.

Set aside specific study times and let your partner know that you need uninterrupted time during those periods. Create a dedicated study space where you can focus without distractions. It might mean investing in noise-canceling headphones or finding a quiet corner in the house.

Also, delegate tasks whenever possible. Enlist your partner, children, or other family members to help with household chores, errands, and childcare. Don't be afraid to ask for help; it's a sign of strength, not weakness. Consider it an opportunity to build a stronger team.

Manage expectations about your performance, too. Law school is tough, and there will be times when you struggle or feel overwhelmed. Don't put undue pressure on yourself to be perfect. Focus on progress, not perfection, and celebrate your accomplishments along the way. Sharing your small victories with your partner can also help them feel more invested in your success.

Another great idea is to involve your partner in your pre-law journey. This can help them feel more connected to your goals and more invested in your success. Share your study materials with them. Explain the concepts you're learning and ask them to quiz you. This can be a fun and engaging way to involve them in your studies and help them understand what you're going through.

Attend pre-law events and information sessions together. This will give your partner a better understanding of the law school application process and the legal profession. It will also allow them to meet other pre-law students and their families, creating a sense of community and support. Maybe they can even make friends with other spouses or partners who are going through the same thing.

If possible, take your partner on a visit to a law school campus. This will give them a firsthand look at the environment you'll be studying in and help them visualize your future. It can make the whole thing feel more real and less abstract.

Also, show your partner the benefits of you going to law school. Point out the good things it will bring to your family's life. Talk about how getting a law degree will make new jobs possible and bring more money into your home.

Share your dreams of how you'll use your law skills to make a positive change and help your community.

Show your partner how attending law school will help them personally. Will it let you give your kids a better education? Will it let you help your parents as they get older? Will it give you more time and money to spend with your loved ones? When you can show the real, good things that will come from your choice, your partner will probably be more willing to support you.

Seek support from other partners who have been through this before. Connect with other partners who are going through or have gone through similar situations.

Join online groups and forums where you can share what's happening, ask questions, and give advice. Go to networking events and meetups for pre-law students and legal workers with families. These connections can give you a sense of friendship and understanding, as well as useful tips and ways to handle your duties.

Don't forget the power of getting help from professionals. Think about hiring a tutor or school coach to help you with the LSAT and the application process. Work with a therapist or counselor to handle stress and keep your mind healthy. Getting help from experts can lighten the load on your family and make sure you have what you need to succeed.

It's also okay to change your plans. The pre-law trip doesn't have to be fast; it can be a slow journey. If you need to take a break to focus on your family or other duties, that's totally fine.

Be open to change and able to adjust. Life happens, and you might need to change your plans along the way. Don't be scared to change your timeline, change your goals, or find other ways to get to law school. The main thing is to stay true to your dream and keep moving forward, even if it's at a slower speed.

Most importantly, remember to take care of yourself. You can't give to others if you have nothing left for yourself. Make sure your body, mind, and feelings are healthy. Plan regular exercise, eat good food, and get enough sleep. Make time for things you enjoy that help you relax and recharge. Practice being aware and kind to yourself. Be gentle with yourself and recognize your wins. Remember that you're trying your best, and that's enough.

When you make yourself a priority, you'll be better able to handle the challenges of the pre-law journey and support your partner along the way.

Think of it as putting on your own oxygen mask before assisting others on a plane.

Going through the pre-law process as a partner is definitely hard, but it can also be really fulfilling. By talking openly, setting expectations, involving your partner, seeking support, and taking care of yourself, you can create an environment of support that helps you follow your dreams and reach your goals. Remember, you're not just working towards a legal career; you're building a better life for yourself and the people you love. That's a win for everyone. It's about creating a shared vision, not just pursuing an individual ambition. And that shared vision starts with getting buy-in early.

Chapter 11: Special Needs- ADHD, Autism, Anxiety, physical disabilities

Tips or dealing with ADHD, Autism and Anxiety

Navigating the pre-law world with special needs like ADHD, autism, or anxiety presents unique hurdles, but it also fosters unique strengths.

ADHD - Your Superpower, Not Your Kryptonite

ADHD, OR ATTENTION-Deficit/Hyperactivity Disorder, often gets a bad rap. People might see the distractibility, the impulsivity, and the seemingly endless energy as weaknesses. But let's reframe that. Those traits, when channeled effectively, can be superpowers in the legal arena.

Understanding Your ADHD:

First, it's vital to really understand your specific ADHD. Not all ADHD is the same. Some individuals primarily struggle with inattention (Difficulty focusing, easily distracted, forgetful), while others are more hyperactive and impulsive (Fidgety, restless, talkative, act without thinking). Many experience a combination of both. A formal diagnosis from a qualified professional (psychologist, psychiatrist) is the first crucial step. This diagnosis opens the door to accommodations, medication options, and, most importantly, a deeper understanding of how your brain works.

Strategies for Thriving:

Embrace Structure (But Make It Flexible): People with ADHD often benefit from structure, but rigid schedules can feel stifling. Find a balance. Use a planner, calendar, or app to schedule study blocks, LSAT prep, and application deadlines. Break down large tasks into smaller, manageable chunks. However, build in flexibility. If you're not feeling a particular task, switch to something else on your list. The goal is to maintain momentum, not force yourself into burnout. Consider time blocking for scheduling out your days.

Hyperfocus to Your Advantage: ADHD can bring intense focus to subjects that truly captivate you – hyperfocus. Identify subjects that genuinely interest you within your pre-law curriculum. If Constitutional Law sets your soul on fire, dive deep. Use that hyperfocus to build a strong foundation. When it comes to less interesting subjects, try to connect them to your passions. Can you find a Constitutional Law angle in a seemingly dry contract case?

Movement is Your Friend: Sitting still for hours on end is torture for someone with ADHD. Don't do it! Incorporate movement into your study routine. Use a standing desk, fidget toy, or take frequent breaks to walk around, stretch, or do a quick workout. Even a few minutes of physical activity can significantly improve focus and concentration. Try using the pomodoro technique (25 mins work, 5 mins break)

Assistive Technology is a Game-Changer: Explore assistive technology. Text-to-speech software can help you process dense reading material. Speech-to-text software can make writing less daunting. Note-taking apps with audio recording can capture lectures and discussions without you having to write everything down. Experiment to find what works best for you.

Accommodations are NOT a Sign of Weakness: If you have a formal ADHD diagnosis, you are entitled to accommodations on the LSAT and in law school. Don't hesitate to request them. Extended time, a separate testing room, or the ability to take breaks can level the playing field and allow you to demonstrate your true potential.

Eliminate Distractions: Identify what distracts you the most and strategically remove those items or influences. If your phone is a distraction, put it in another room. If notifications distract you, turn them off.

Autism - Unique Perspectives, Unique Strengths

AUTISM SPECTRUM DISORDER (ASD) is a neurodevelopmental condition characterized by differences in social interaction, communication, and behavior. Again, autism is a spectrum. Individuals with autism possess a wide range of abilities and challenges.

Understanding Your Autism:

Self-awareness is key. Understand your sensory sensitivities (e.g., noise, light, textures), your communication style, and your preferred learning methods. This understanding allows you to advocate for your needs and create an environment where you can thrive. Many people with autism have a strong focus and the ability to see patterns, which can be helpful for law school.

Strategies for Thriving

Leverage Your Pattern Recognition Skills: Many individuals with autism possess exceptional pattern recognition skills. This is invaluable for the LSAT, which is heavily based on logic and identifying flaws in arguments. Practice logic games and reading comprehension passages, focusing on identifying underlying structures and relationships.

Create Predictable Routines: Predictability can reduce anxiety and improve focus. Establish consistent study routines, including specific times, locations, and materials. Minimize unexpected changes to your schedule. If changes are unavoidable, prepare yourself in advance.

Communicate Your Needs Clearly: Don't be afraid to communicate your needs to professors, classmates, and potential recommenders. If you have difficulty with eye contact, explain that. If you need written instructions instead of verbal ones, ask for them. Clear communication prevents misunderstandings and ensures you receive the support you need.

Advocate for Sensory Accommodations: If you are sensitive to noise, request a quiet study space in the library. If you are bothered by fluorescent lighting, wear sunglasses or ask if the lighting can be adjusted. If certain textures are uncomfortable, choose clothing and seating that are comfortable for you.

Social Skills Support: Law school is inherently social, so make sure to practice your social skills. Start small by practicing ordering in a restaurant. Then, meet a few new people and practice starting a conversation. If social skills are a challenge, consider social skills training or support groups. Practice with a trusted friend or family member.

Find Your Niche: Law is a vast field. Explore different areas of law to find one that aligns with your interests and strengths. Perhaps you are drawn to intellectual property law, where attention to detail and technical expertise are highly valued. Or maybe you are passionate about disability rights law, where your personal experiences can inform your advocacy.

Anxiety - Taming the Worry Beast

ANXIETY IS A COMMON experience, but for some, it can be debilitating. The pre-law process, with its inherent uncertainty and pressure, can exacerbate anxiety.

Understanding Your Anxiety:

Recognize your anxiety triggers. What situations or thoughts tend to spark your anxiety? Is it the LSAT, the personal statement, the fear of rejection? Once you identify your triggers, you can develop coping mechanisms. A formal diagnosis from a mental health professional can help you to determine the root of your anxiety.

Strategies for Thriving:

Mindfulness and Meditation: Mindfulness and meditation techniques can help you to calm your mind and reduce anxiety. Practice deep breathing exercises, focusing on the present moment. There are many free apps and online resources that can guide you through meditation practices.

Cognitive Behavioral Therapy (CBT): CBT is a type of therapy that helps you to identify and change negative thought patterns. It can be an effective tool for managing anxiety. Consider working with a therapist trained in CBT.

Challenge Negative Thoughts: When you experience anxious thoughts, challenge them. Ask yourself: Is this thought based on facts or feelings? Is there another way to look at the situation? What is the worst-case scenario, and how likely is it to happen?

Break Down Tasks: Anxiety can be overwhelming. Break down large tasks into smaller, more manageable steps. Focus on completing one step at a time. Celebrate your accomplishments along the way.

Build a Support System: Connect with friends, family, or other pre-law students who can offer support and encouragement. Share your anxieties and fears with them. Talking about your feelings can help you to feel less alone and more in control.

Prioritize Self-Care: When you're feeling anxious, it's easy to neglect self-care. Make time for activities that you enjoy and that help you to relax. Get enough sleep, eat healthy foods, and exercise regularly. Even small acts of self-care can make a big difference.

LSAT Anxiety Techniques: The LSAT can be scary. Build in strategies to alleviate anxiety to help you do your best on the test.

Remember, navigating the pre-law journey with special needs may require some extra planning and effort, but it is absolutely achievable. By understanding your unique strengths and challenges, implementing effective strategies, and seeking support when needed, you can thrive and achieve your legal aspirations. You got this.

Tips for Dealing with Physical Disabilities

FOR THOSE NAVIGATING the pre-law journey with physical disabilities, success requires acknowledging challenges and actively crafting strategies to overcome them.

Understanding Your Needs:

The first step is profound self-awareness. Recognize the specific ways your physical disability impacts your daily life, study habits, and ability to navigate the world. Are there mobility challenges? Do you experience chronic pain or fatigue? Are there limitations to fine motor skills? The more clearly you understand your needs, the better equipped you will be to advocate for yourself and find appropriate solutions.

Consider these questions:

- What are your physical limitations?
- How does your disability impact your ability to study, attend classes, and take exams?
- What accommodations do you require to fully participate in the pre-law process?
- What support systems do you have in place?

Strategies for Thriving:

Accessibility is Non-Negotiable: Ensure physical accessibility in all aspects of your pre-law journey. This includes accessible classrooms, libraries, and study spaces. Investigate the accessibility features of potential law schools early in the application process. Don't hesitate to contact the disability services office at each school to inquire about specific accommodations and support services.

Assistive Technology is Your Ally: Embrace assistive technology to overcome physical limitations. Speech-to-text software can ease the burden of writing. Text-to-speech software can assist with reading. Specialized keyboards and mice can improve computer access. Explore the wide range of assistive technology options available and find the tools that work best for you.

Time Management is Crucial: Chronic pain and fatigue can make it challenging to maintain a consistent study schedule. Prioritize time management and break down large tasks into smaller, more manageable chunks. Schedule frequent breaks to rest and recharge. Be realistic about what you can accomplish in a given day and avoid overcommitting yourself.

Advocate for Accommodations: Don't be afraid to advocate for yourself and request the accommodations you need to succeed. This may include extended time on exams, note-taking assistance, preferential seating, or alternative testing formats. Familiarize yourself with the legal rights of students with disabilities and be prepared to assert those rights if necessary. The Americans with Disabilities Act (ADA) protects students with disabilities from discrimination and ensures that they have equal access to educational opportunities.

Build a Strong Support System: Surround yourself with a supportive network of friends, family, mentors, and other pre-law students. Share your challenges and successes with others. Seek out role models who have successfully navigated the legal profession with a disability.

Prioritize Self-Care: Taking care of your physical and mental health is essential for managing chronic pain and fatigue. Get enough sleep, eat healthy foods, and exercise regularly. Practice relaxation techniques such as yoga, meditation, or deep breathing. Engage in activities that bring you joy and help you to de-stress.

Manage Pain and Fatigue: Develop strategies for managing pain and fatigue. This may include medication, physical therapy, occupational therapy, or alternative therapies such as acupuncture or massage. Learn to recognize your early warning signs of pain and fatigue and take steps to prevent flare-ups.

Transportation Planning: Depending on the physical disability, try to plan transportation in advance and utilize accessible options. Try to map out an accessible route if needed.

Emotional Support: Seeking counseling to deal with emotional issues will help. Having a physical disability can lead to a variety of issues such as depression, anxiety or stress.

Ergonomic Considerations: Ensure your study space is ergonomically sound to avoid strain and discomfort. Adjust your chair, desk, and computer monitor to promote good posture. Use a supportive keyboard and mouse. Take frequent breaks to stretch and move around.

Flexibility is Key: Be prepared to adapt your plans as needed. Some days, you may be able to accomplish more than others. Be flexible with your schedule and prioritize tasks based on your energy levels. Don't be afraid to ask for help when you need it.

Connect with Disability Organizations: There are many organizations that provide support and resources for people with disabilities. Connect with these organizations to learn about scholarships, internships, and mentorship opportunities.

Disclose Strategically: Decide when and how to disclose your disability to law schools. You are not required to disclose your disability, but doing so may allow you to receive accommodations and support services.

Reframing Perceptions: Help others understand your disability and the accommodations you need. Be patient and persistent in educating others about disability awareness.

Resources for Students with Disabilities:
The National Disabled Law Students Association

The National Disabled Law Students Association (NDLSA) is a powerful resource for aspiring lawyers with disabilities or chronic conditions. NDLSA creates community, advocacy, and support for law students navigating accessibility issues, accommodations, and inclusion in legal education. Pre-law students can benefit by connecting early, exploring NDLSA's website, joining their virtual events, or following their social media platforms to learn about resources, mentorship opportunities, and guidance on requesting accommodations during the LSAT and law school application process. Tapping into NDLSA before you start law school gives you insider knowledge, a supportive network, and the confidence to advocate for yourself from day one.

The American Association of People with Disabilities (AAPD): AAPD is a national organization that advocates for the rights of people with disabilities. They offer a variety of programs and resources for students with disabilities, including scholarships, internships, and mentorship opportunities.

The Disability Rights Education & Defense Fund (DREDF): DREDF is a national law and policy center that advocates for the civil and human rights of people with disabilities. They provide legal assistance and training to students with disabilities.

The National Disability Rights Network (NDRN): NDRN is a national network of protection and advocacy agencies that provide legal assistance and advocacy to people with disabilities.

Job Accommodation Network (JAN): JAN is a free consulting service that provides information about job accommodations and the Americans with Disabilities Act (ADA).

Recording for the Blind & Dyslexic (RFB&D): RFB&D provides accessible educational materials to students with disabilities.

Remember, your physical disability does not define you. It is simply one aspect of your identity. With the right strategies, accommodations, and support systems, you can overcome challenges and achieve your legal aspirations. Believe in yourself and never give up on your dreams. You bring a unique perspective and valuable experiences to the legal profession.

Law School Specific Strategies:

Visit Law Schools: Visit the law schools you're interested in to assess their physical accessibility. Can you easily navigate the buildings, classrooms, library, and other essential areas? Are there accessible restrooms and elevators?

Talk to Current Students: Connect with current law students with disabilities. Ask about their experiences with accommodations, support services, and the overall campus climate.

Engage with Disability Services: Meet with the disability services office at each law school to discuss your specific needs and explore the accommodations available.

Scholarships and Financial Aid: Many scholarships and financial aid opportunities are specifically for students with disabilities. Research and apply for these resources to help finance your legal education.

Consider Online Programs: Online law school programs may be a viable option if physical accessibility is a significant concern. Ensure the program is reputable and offers adequate support services.

Building Mental Toughness:

Challenge Limiting Beliefs: Confront any negative beliefs or self-doubt related to your disability. Focus on your strengths and abilities.

Practice Resilience: Develop coping mechanisms for dealing with setbacks and disappointments. Remember that resilience is a skill that can be learned and strengthened over time.

Celebrate Small Victories: Acknowledge and celebrate your accomplishments, no matter how small. This will help you to maintain motivation and build self-confidence.

Visualize Success: Imagine yourself thriving in law school and in your legal career. Visualization can help you to overcome anxiety and stay focused on your goals.

The pre-law journey may present unique obstacles for individuals with physical disabilities, but it is far from insurmountable. By proactively addressing accessibility needs, leveraging assistive technology, building strong support systems, and cultivating mental toughness, you can pave the way for a rewarding and successful legal career. Embrace your unique strengths and perspectives, and never let your disability define your potential.

Chapter 12: Conclusion

Walk In Like You Own It

Law school isn't the finish line—it's just the next starting point in your legal journey. After all the preparation, applications, and waiting, you'll finally walk through those law school doors. But how you enter matters almost as much as getting in.

The BE§T MODE approach isn't something you discard once you receive your acceptance letters. It's an operating system that will continue to serve you throughout law school and your legal career. The habits, mindset, and strategies you've developed during your pre-law journey have prepared you not just to survive law school, but to thrive there.

Entering with Confidence

True confidence isn't about knowing everything, it's about trusting your ability to handle challenges as they arise. You've already proven your resilience through the demanding application process. Remember:

- Your acceptance wasn't a mistake or luck—you earned your place.
- Everyone around you is experiencing similar doubts and uncertainties.
- The skills that got you admitted are the same ones that will help you succeed.
- You don't need to be the loudest voice in the room to be impactful.

This confidence should be balanced with humility. Law school will challenge you in new ways, and recognizing when you need help is a strength, not a weakness.

Maintaining Authenticity

Law school can pressure students to conform to a certain mold or persona. Resist this pressure:

- Your unique background and perspective are assets to the legal profession.
- The most memorable and effective lawyers bring their authentic selves to their work.
- Trying to become someone else consumes energy better spent on learning.
- Your authentic voice will help you connect with clients, colleagues, and judges.

This doesn't mean refusing to adapt or grow. It means evolving while staying true to your core values and identity.

Preparedness Beyond Academics

Academic preparation is just one component of law school readiness. You're also prepared for:

The emotional journey:

- You've developed self-compassion practices for difficult days.
- You understand the importance of celebrating small wins.
- You've built resilience through LSAT preparation and application challenges.
- You know how to manage imposter syndrome when it arises.

The physical demands:

- You've established sustainable health routines that support cognitive function.
- You understand the connection between sleep, nutrition, and academic performance.
- You've created exercise habits that can adapt to a busy schedule.
- You recognize the warning signs of burnout and know how to respond.

The social dynamics:

- You've practiced professional communication with professors and mentors.
- You understand how to build meaningful connections without getting caught in comparison.
- You've learned to identify supportive versus draining relationships.
- You know how to contribute to a community while maintaining boundaries.

BE§T MODE as an Ongoing Operating System

The components of BE§T MODE will continue to serve you:

Believe in Your Calling:

- Your "why" will sustain you through difficult courses and challenging career decisions.
- Your affirmations will evolve to address new challenges.
- Your vision of success will expand beyond grades to professional impact.

Eliminate Distractions:

- The boundaries you've set will help you navigate the many demands on your time.
- Your focus-first environment will adapt to new study locations.
- Your ability to identify energy drains will help you manage law school social dynamics.

Set the Foundation and Strategize:

- Your strategic approach to course selection will apply to law school electives.
- Your relationship-building skills will help you connect with professors and potential employers.
- Your grade management strategies will transfer to the unique challenges of law school assessment.

Train Consistently:

- The study habits you developed for the LSAT will serve you in exam preparation.
- Your test-taking mindset will help you approach law school exams strategically.
- Your ability to analyze mistakes and adapt will support continuous improvement.

Master Your Mindset:

- Your emotional fitness will help you navigate the stress of cold calls and exams.
- Your mental obstacle management will address new challenges as they arise.
- Your self-compassion practices will sustain you through inevitable setbacks.

Open Doors Before Closing:

1. Your networking skills will help you build relationships with practicing attorneys.
2. Your professional communication abilities will set you apart in internship applications.
3. Your proactive approach to opportunities will continue to create options for your career.

Design Your Health Strategy:

- Your meal planning systems will support your wellbeing during busy periods.
- Your sustainable exercise routines will adapt to your law school schedule.
- Your sleep prioritization will maintain your cognitive performance.

Elevate Your Game:

- Your ability to present yourself effectively will transfer to job interviews and networking events.
- Your strategic approach to opportunities will help you make the most of law school resources.
- Your authentic voice will help you stand out in a competitive environment.

Consider Malik, who felt overwhelmed during his first week of law school until he realized he already had the tools to succeed. He returned to the BE§T MODE strategies he'd developed during his pre-law journey—setting boundaries around social media, maintaining his morning exercise routine, using his affirmations before difficult classes, and reaching out proactively to professors. By the end of his first semester, he wasn't just surviving—he was thriving.

You've done more than prepare for law school admission, you've built a foundation for legal excellence. Now walk through those law school doors like you own the place, because you've earned the right to be there. Your journey is just beginning, and you're ready for whatever comes next.

Thirty Day Challenge

HERE'S THE THING: GETTING ready for law school shouldn't feel like running a marathon without training. It should be about leveling up, step by strategic step. That's why I created the "30 Days to BE§T MODE" Challenge – a guided tour to get your mind, habits, and application materials in tip-top shape. This isn't about cramming; it's about building momentum.

Before You Dive In

Think of this challenge as a personalized workout plan. What are your weak spots? What areas make you feel insecure? Are you solid on the LSAT, but your resume looks sad? Or do you know you need to make some changes to your health habits? Before you start day one, take a hard look at where you stand. Use the planner printable provided, tailor it to your needs.

The Challenge: Your 30-Day Roadmap

Here's your daily dose of BE§T Mode. Remember, consistency beats intensity.

Week 1: Mindset Makeover

- **Day 1: Identify Your "Why."** Spend 30 minutes journaling. Dig deep: Why law school? What impact do you want to make? Use the "Five Whys" technique: Ask "why" five times to get to the root of your motivation. Write it down. Post it somewhere you'll see it daily.
- **Day 2: Visualization Power-Up.** Close your eyes. Picture yourself succeeding in law school. What does it feel like? What are you doing? Run through this movie in your head for 10 minutes. It sounds cheesy, but it works to quiet the mind and help to reduce anxiety.
- **Day 3: Affirmation Time.** Craft three personalized affirmations. For example: "I am capable of mastering the LSAT," or "I am a strong candidate for law school." Write them down five times each. Say them out loud with conviction. Do you feel like you are lying? That's alright, keep at it!
- **Day 4: Social Media Audit.** Track your social media usage for a day. Be honest. Which apps suck up your time? Where are you mindlessly scrolling? Note the triggers.

- **Day 5: Digital Detox.** Implement a "no social media before noon" rule. Replace that wasted time with something productive: reading, exercise, or LSAT prep. Or sleeping in!
- **Day 6: Energy Vampire Check.** Identify one "energy vampire" in your life – someone who consistently drains your motivation. Brainstorm ways to limit your contact with this person or set stronger boundaries.
- **Day 7: Gratitude Journaling.** Write down three things you're grateful for. It could be anything – a supportive friend, a sunny day, a small victory. This helps shift your focus to the positive.

Week 2: Strategic Foundation Building

- **Day 8: Course Review.** Evaluate your past coursework. Which classes genuinely challenged you and built relevant skills (writing, analysis, critical thinking)? How can you build on those skills this semester?
- **Day 9: Professor Connection.** Identify a professor you admire. Schedule a brief office hours visit to discuss your interest in law school and ask for advice. Even if you don't click with them, you lost nothing.
- **Day 10: Recommender Relationship.** Send a thank-you note to a professor who has positively influenced you. Briefly mention your law school aspirations and express your appreciation for their guidance. Start cultivating the relationship early.
- **Day 11: GPA Reality Check.** Calculate your current GPA. Are you where you need to be? If not, identify one concrete step you can take to improve your grades this semester.
- **Day 12: Budget Basics.** Research the average cost of living in a city where you might want to attend law school. Use the tools available from AccessLex or another cost-of-living calculator.
- **Day 13: Financial Aid Deep Dive.** Research one law school scholarship you might be eligible for. Note the requirements and deadlines.
- **Day 14: Savings Plan.** Identify one small expense you can cut from

your budget each week and put that money into a savings account earmarked for law school.

Week 3: LSAT Domination

- **Day 15: LSAT Diagnostic.** Take a full-length, timed LSAT diagnostic test (using official LSAT questions!). No excuses. This is your baseline. Analyze your results carefully. Which sections are your strengths? Your weaknesses?
- **Day 16: Learning Style Assessment.** Reflect on how you learn best. Are you a visual learner? Do you prefer reading or interactive exercises? Choose LSAT prep resources that align with your style.
- **Day 17: Resource Gathering.** Research three LSAT prep resources (books, courses, online programs). Compare costs, features, and reviews. Select the one that best fits your budget and learning style.
- **Day 18: Study Schedule.** Create a realistic LSAT study schedule, allocating specific days and times for studying each week. Be specific! Don't just say "study LSAT." Say, "7-9 PM: Logical Reasoning drills."
- **Day 19: Logical Reasoning Focus.** Dedicate today to Logical Reasoning. Review key concepts (argument structure, common fallacies). Complete a set of timed practice questions.
- **Day 20: Reading Comprehension.** Practice speed-reading techniques. Read a complex article and summarize the main points in your own words. Then, tackle a Reading Comprehension passage from an LSAT practice test.
- **Day 21: Analytical Reasoning.** Drill logic games. Focus on mastering one game type. Time yourself. Analyze your mistakes.

Week 4: Application Polish and Wellness Boost

- **Day 22: Personal Statement Brainstorm.** Spend 30 minutes brainstorming potential personal statement topics. What experiences have shaped your interest in law? What unique qualities do you bring to the table? Don't self-censor. Just write.
- **Day 23: Resume Refresh.** Update your resume, highlighting your

academic achievements, analytical skills, and leadership experiences. Use the CAR (Challenge, Action, Result) method to showcase your accomplishments.

- **Day 24: Recommendation Letter Strategy.** Make a list of potential recommenders. Who knows you well and can speak to your strengths? Draft a brief email template to request a letter of recommendation.
- **Day 25: Pre-Law Program Research.** Research one pre-law program or internship that interests you (CLEO, SEO Law, etc.). Note the application requirements and deadlines.
- **Day 26: Networking Outreach.** Connect with one legal professional on LinkedIn. Send a personalized message expressing your interest in their career path and asking for advice.
- **Day 27: Meal Prep Power.** Dedicate an hour to meal prepping healthy lunches and snacks for the week. Focus on brain-boosting foods like fruits, vegetables, and lean protein.
- **Day 28: Exercise Recharge.** Schedule a workout you enjoy – yoga, running, dancing, weightlifting. Move your body for at least 30 minutes.
- **Day 29: Sleep Sanctuary.** Create a relaxing bedtime routine. Take a warm bath, read a book, or listen to calming music. Aim for 7-8 hours of quality sleep.
- **Day 30: Reflection and Celebration.** Review your progress over the past 30 days. What have you accomplished? What have you learned? Celebrate your commitment to yourself and your future legal career. What is your reward?

Important Considerations Throughout the Challenge:

- **Flexibility is Key:** Life happens. Don't beat yourself up if you miss a day. Just get back on track the next day. The point is to build momentum, not achieve perfection.
- **Listen to Your Body:** If you're feeling burned out, take a break. Rest and recharge. This is a marathon, not a sprint.
- **Seek Support:** Connect with other pre-law students. Share your

struggles and successes. Find a mentor or accountability partner.

- **Track Your Progress:** Use a journal, spreadsheet, or app to track your progress. Seeing your accomplishments will keep you motivated.
- **Don't Compare Yourself to Others:** Everyone's journey is unique. Focus on your own goals and celebrate your own achievements.
- **Embrace the Process:** The pre-law journey is challenging, but it can also be incredibly rewarding. Embrace the process, learn from your mistakes, and enjoy the ride.
- **Ask for help:** Call a friend, or family member. Even if it is just to vent, just make sure they are the right people.

Customization is Important Too

The 30-Day Challenge is designed to be a starting point. Don't be afraid to customize it to fit your individual needs and goals.

- **If you're already strong in one area,** spend less time on those tasks and focus on areas where you need more improvement.
- **If you have more time,** add additional tasks to each day.
- **If you have less time,** break down the tasks into smaller, more manageable chunks.

The most important thing is to find a system that works for you and that you can stick with. This is YOUR journey to BE§T MODE.

Beyond the 30 Days

The 30-Day Challenge is just the beginning. The skills and habits you develop during this challenge will serve you well throughout the entire pre-law process and beyond. Continue to use the BE§T Mode mindset to guide your decisions and actions. Stay focused on your goals, stay positive, and never give up on your dreams.

And remember, this journey is not just about getting into law school. It's about becoming the best version of yourself – a confident, resilient, and successful future lawyer. You got this.

Appendix: Pre-Law Reading List

You don't need to read every book on this list before applying to law school. Instead:

- Start with one book from each category that addresses your most pressing needs.
- Read actively, taking notes on key concepts and how they apply to your pre-law journey.
- Implement one new idea from each book before moving to the next.
- Return to these books at different stages of your pre-law and law school journey.
- Consider forming a study group to discuss these books with other pre-law students.

Remember, the goal isn't just to read these books but to apply their insights to develop the thinking patterns, habits, and mindsets that will serve you throughout your legal career.

10 Essential Books for Pre-Law Students

1. Haben: The Deafblind Woman Who Conquered Harvard Law by Haben Girma

Haben Girma, the first Deafblind graduate of Harvard Law School, shares her story of resilience, advocacy, and innovation. Her memoir is a blueprint for perseverance and using law as a tool for inclusion and justice.

2. Sister Outsider by Audre Lorde

A collection of essays and speeches by Black feminist writer Audre Lorde. It's a masterclass in critical thinking, intersectionality, and advocacy—skills every future lawyer needs.

3. *Limitless: Upgrade Your Brain, Learn Anything Faster, and Unlock Your Exceptional Life by Jim Kwik*

A practical guide on speed reading, memory, and focus. Perfect for prepping your brain for the heavy reading and memorization law school demands.

4. *Grit: The Power of Passion and Perseverance by Angela Duckworth*

Law school isn't just about raw intellect—it's about persistence. This book teaches resilience, discipline, and the long game.

5. *Bird by Bird: Some Instructions on Writing and Life by Anne Lamott*

A classic on writing clearly and with heart. If you want to strengthen your essays, memos, and even personal statements, Lamott's wisdom will serve you well.

6. *They Say / I Say: The Moves That Matter in Academic Writing by Gerald Graff and Cathy Birkenstein*

This slim, practical text breaks down how to argue effectively in writing—a foundational skill for legal briefs and law school exams.

7. *Generations: The Real Differences Between Gen Z, Millennials, Gen X, Boomers, and Silents—and What They Mean for America's Future by Jean M. Twenge, Ph.D.*

Great for understanding generational perspectives, which show up in classrooms, workplaces, and even juries. Pre-law students benefit from seeing how different cohorts think and communicate.

8. *Law School Confidential by Robert H. Miller*

A frank, detailed guide to how law school actually works, written by a Harvard Law grad. It demystifies case briefing, cold calls, and why law school is nothing like undergrad or even a master's program.

9. *Minority Mentor: Navigating Law School and Beyond by Meera E. Deo*

Written by a woman of color law professor, this book gives strategies for minority and first-generation students to succeed in a system not designed for them.

10. *Letter to a Young Female Physician: Notes from a Medical Life by Suzanne Koven, M.D.*

Though about medicine, this memoir resonates with law students—the pressures of professional school, imposter syndrome, and finding your voice in a demanding field. A powerful read on resilience and identity.

Appendix: Email Script Templates

These templates provide starting points for common pre-law communication scenarios. Customize them with your specific details and situation while maintaining the professional tone and structure.

These are designed to be direct, professional, and easy to customize. Remember to always tailor them to your specific situation and the person you're contacting.

Here are some email script templates:

Template 1: Informational Interview Request (Networking)

Subject: Request to Learn About [Area of Law/Company/Organization] from [Name of Professional]

Dear [Mr./Ms./Mx. Last Name],

My name is [Your Name], and I'm a [Year] at [Your University] studying [Your Major]. I'm reaching out because I'm really interested in [Area of Law/Company/Organization], and your experience at [Place of Work/Organization] is truly impressive.

I'm exploring career paths in law, and I'm eager to learn more about what a career in [Area of Law] looks like day-to-day. I was particularly intrigued by [Specific project, article, or aspect of their work – show you've done your research].

Would you be open to a brief informational interview, perhaps 20-30 minutes, where I could ask about your experiences and gain some insights? I'm available on [List a couple of specific dates/times]. Of course, I'm happy to work around your schedule.

Thank you for considering my request. I truly appreciate your time and guidance.

Sincerely,

[Your Name]
[Your Email Address]
[Your Phone Number (Optional)]

Why this works:

- **Personalization:** It shows you've done your homework on the person you're contacting.
- **Clear Ask:** It's direct about what you want (an informational interview) and the time commitment involved.
- **Flexibility:** It offers to work around their schedule.
- **Gratitude:** It expresses appreciation for their time.

How to customize:

- Replace bracketed information with specific details.
- Mention a specific connection you have (e.g., "I was referred to you by...").
- Highlight a particular skill or experience they have that you admire.

Template 2: Following Up After Networking Event

Subject: Following Up – [Event Name] – [Your Name]

Dear [Mr./Ms./Mx. Last Name],

It was a pleasure meeting you at [Event Name] on [Date]. I truly enjoyed our conversation about [Specific topic you discussed]. I especially appreciated your insights on [Specific point they made].

As we discussed, I'm very interested in [Area of Law] and am actively exploring opportunities to learn more. Your experience at [Company/Organization] sounds very interesting, and I admire your approach to [Specific aspect].

Thank you again for your time and for sharing your expertise. I hope to stay in touch.

Sincerely,

[Your Name]
[Your Email Address]
[Your Phone Number (Optional)]

Why this works:

- **Memory Jogger:** It reminds them where and when you met.
- **Specificity:** It mentions a specific topic you discussed, showing you were engaged.
- **Gratitude:** It expresses appreciation for their time and expertise.
- **Call to action (subtle):** It signals your interest in staying connected.

How to customize:

- If you promised to send them something (e.g., your resume, an article), include it.
- If they offered to connect you with someone, subtly remind them. For example: "I also wanted to follow up on your kind offer to connect me with [Name]."
- Consider adding them on LinkedIn and referencing that in the email.

Template 3: Internship Application Follow-Up

Subject: Following Up on Internship Application – [Your Name] – [Position Name]

Dear [Hiring Manager Name or "Hiring Team"],

I am writing to follow up on my application for the [Position Name] internship, which I submitted on [Date]. I am very enthusiastic about this opportunity and eager to contribute to [Company/Organization].

Since submitting my application, I [mention any relevant new developments, e.g., completed a relevant project, attended a relevant workshop, etc.]. I am confident that my skills and experiences in [List 2-3 relevant skills] align well with the requirements outlined in the job description.

Thank you for your time and consideration. I am available for an interview at your earliest convenience.

Sincerely,

[Your Name]

[Your Email Address]

[Your Phone Number]

Why this works:

- **Professional Tone:** It's polite and respectful.
- **Enthusiasm:** It shows you're still interested in the position.
- **Value Add:** It highlights new developments or reinforces your qualifications.
- **Call to Action:** It makes it clear you're available for an interview.

How to customize:

- If you know the hiring manager's name, use it. If not, research to find it.
- Quantify your achievements whenever possible (e.g., "Increased efficiency by 15%...").
- Tailor the skills you highlight to match the specific requirements of the internship.

Template 4: Requesting a Recommendation Letter (Professor/ Supervisor)

Subject: Recommendation Request – [Your Name] – Law School Application

Dear [Professor/Supervisor's Last Name],

I hope this email finds you well.

I am writing to request a letter of recommendation in support of my application to law school. I am planning to apply to law schools this [Fall/ Summer/Winter] for admission in [Year].

I truly enjoyed your [Course Name] class [or "my time working under your supervision"]. I particularly appreciated [mention a specific assignment, project, or interaction that stood out]. Your guidance on [Specific skill or concept] was instrumental in [Positive outcome].

To help you write a strong letter, I have attached the following materials:

- My resume
- My personal statement (draft)
- A transcript of my grades
- A list of the law schools I am applying to, along with deadlines
- A brief reminder sheet highlighting key accomplishments and

experiences relevant to my law school applications

Please let me know if you are able to write a letter on my behalf by [Date – give them at least 2-3 weeks]. The deadline for most of my applications is [Date]. If you are unable to write a letter, I completely understand.

Thank you for your time and consideration.

Sincerely,

[Your Name]

[Your Email Address]

[Your Phone Number]

Why this works:

- **Polite and Respectful:** It starts with a polite greeting and expresses gratitude.
- **Clear Request:** It clearly states what you're asking for.
- **Context:** It provides background information about your application plans.
- **Helpful Materials:** It includes all the necessary materials to make writing the letter easier.
- **Reasonable Deadline:** It gives the recommender ample time to write the letter.
- **Graceful Exit:** It allows them to decline without feeling pressured.

How to customize:

- Personalize the email with specific details about your experience with the professor/supervisor.
- In the "reminder sheet," highlight specific skills and qualities you want them to emphasize in the letter.
- If possible, ask in person before sending the email.

Template 5: Thank You Note After Recommendation Letter Submission

Subject: Thank you for writing my letter of recommendation

Dear [Professor/Supervisor's Last Name],

I am writing to express my sincere gratitude for writing a letter of recommendation in support of my application to law school. I really appreciate you taking the time to do this, especially with all your other commitments.

I know these letters can be time-consuming, and I can't tell you how much I appreciate you sharing your experience and your willingness to advocate for me.

Thanks to you, I feel more confident about my applications to law school. Thank you again for your support.

Sincerely,

[Your Name]

[Your Email Address]

[Your Phone Number]

Why this works:

- **Timeliness:** Send the letter as soon as you're notified.
- **Sincerity:** This cannot be overstated.
- **Acknowledgement:** Acknowledge their time and commitment.

How to customize:

- You can add how excited and nervous you are to go through the process.
- Include a bit about your plans for the future.

General Tips for All Email Templates:

- **Proofread carefully:** Before sending any email, double-check for typos and grammatical errors.
- **Use a professional email address:** Avoid using unprofessional or silly email addresses.
- **Keep it concise:** Get to the point quickly and avoid rambling.
- **Use a clear subject line:** Make it easy for the recipient to understand the purpose of your email.
- **Be polite and respectful:** Use professional language and tone.
- **Follow up (if necessary):** If you don't receive a response within a

reasonable timeframe (e.g., a week), send a polite follow-up email.

By using these templates as a starting point and customizing them to your specific needs, you can effectively communicate with professionals, build your network, and strengthen your law school applications.

Don't miss out!

Visit the website below and you can sign up to receive emails whenever Joseline Jean-Louis Hardrick publishes a new book. There's no charge and no obligation.

https://books2read.com/r/B-A-HBUXD-VGOVG

BOOKS 2 READ

Connecting independent readers to independent writers.

Also by Joseline Jean-Louis Hardrick

In Their Own Time Understanding the World Through the Eyes of Our Children

The Tao of Us A Divine Feminine Reflection on the Tao Te Ching

Whispers of Wisdom: A Divine Feminine Reflection on The Book of Proverbs

Pre Law Best Mode Strategies to Win Before Law School Even Begins

Watch for more at www.joselinehardrick.com.

About the Author

Joseline Jean-Louis Hardrick is a lawyer, professor, storyteller, and seeker of balance in all things. Blending the discipline of law with the flow of poetry, she reimagines ancient wisdom for modern lives. Her work bridges cultures, generations, and worlds—inviting readers to find stillness in the swirl, strength in the soft, and joy in the journey.

Read more at www.joselinehardrick.com.

LAWYERISH®

EMPOWERING EVERY LEGAL JOURNEY

About the Publisher

Lawyerish®

Empowering Every Legal Journey™

At Lawyerish®, we empower the next generation of legal professionals by meeting them where they are and guiding them to where they want to go. Connect with us at lawyerish.org. Lawyerish® is a registered trademark of Twelve:Two Training, LLC.

Read more at https://www.lawyerish.org.